101 Hotel
Lobbies, Bars
& Restaurants

101 Hotel
Lobbies, Bars & Restaurants

Corinna Kretschmar-Joehnk
Peter Joehnk

BRAUN

Contents

Preface
by Corinna Kretschmar-Joehnk and Peter Joehnk

Following the success of our first publication – *101 Hotel Rooms* – this new book explores public areas in hospitality. Showcasing JOI-Design's best work in this area, *101 Hotel-Lobbies, Bars & Restaurants* reviews a broad spectrum of design solutions for interiors that can make or break a hotel experience.

Given the increasingly important role of hotel lobbies, bars and restaurants, the authors have tracked developments in public area design for a number of years, observing the shifts in hotel interior design as it responds to the rapid pace of change that distinguishes contemporary society. We have tracked developments in public area design for a number of years, observing the shifts in hotel interior design as it responds to the rapid pace of change that distinguishes contemporary society.

Public areas are the showpieces of every hotel – barometers of style, they reveal every change in trends and fashion. Guests respond to these interiors at an intuitive level: there are no second chances when it comes to first impressions.

What do these interiors reveal? In a world of ubiquitous 24/7 access and availability, guests yearn for interiors that exude an aura of authenticity, individuality and natural appeal – values which contrast with those of the digital world with its never-ending stream of updates and information. This desire represents a return to the values of an earlier age. Purely decorative designs that operate exclusively at the surface level have fallen from favor. Today's interiors must have soul and character. These qualities lend interiors credibility and create narratives that guests will embrace and make their own. In interior design, it's often the discoveries we make at a second glance which fill us with wonder and delight. It is to such places that we return again and again.

We trust that our more observant readers will forgive our decision to feature 110 projects rather than the 101 suggested by the title - there was simply so much that we wanted to share!

AC Hotel Ambassadeur
Juan-les-Pins, France

Lobby

Hotel Category: ★ ★ ★ ★ ★

Hotel Type: Resort and conference hotel

Size: 221 rooms

The Brief: Renovation: development of a design concept for the lobby

Total floor space: 98.70 m²

Seats: 12

The Mediterranean sun, scented pine groves and seaside living coupled with the irresistible rhythms of a soothing jazz melody – all the perfect ingredients for one unforgettable summer evening after the next in the enchanted town of Juan-les-Pins on the French Riviera. Natural materials and colors with a strong regional flavor transport this atmosphere into the hotel's interior. But ultimately it's the hotel's fine accent furnishings that will make a lasting impression.

Guests are welcomed into the hotel by the lobby with its delicate color scheme and sophisticated reception corner clad in crème leather complemented by wood accents in red and brown hues. The same lush teak surfaces adorn the wall backing the reception. Playing on the hotel's maritime location, the gentle curves spanning these wall panels evoke associations with a ship's hull. This theme is continued in the table lamps illuminating the corners, whose glass bodies are akin to intertwined mooring lines.

Maritime elegance under the Mediterranean sun.

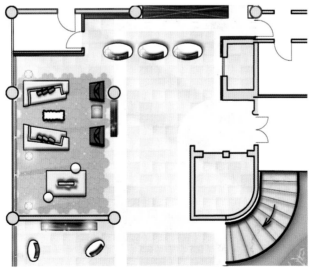

AC Hotel Ambassadeur
Juan-les-Pins, France

Bar

Hotel Category: ★ ★ ★ ★ ★

Hotel Type: Resort and conference hotel

Size: 221 rooms

The Brief: Renovation: development of a design concept for the bar

Total floor space: 169.85 m²

Seats: 54

Hotel bars have many roles to play – depending on the time of day, they are a place to relax for five minutes and read a newspaper, somewhere to meet before embarking on the next excursion, a venue for a casual business appointment or a glass or two of wine in good company of an evening. This bar is a genuine crowd-pleaser that knows its job. It features a variety of seating options, qualities and heights, together with an intelligent lighting concept and a multi-purpose design that will appeal to business and leisure guests alike. Custom design details make for an atmosphere of welcoming sophistication. The suspended light fittings floating above the bar counter make for an eye-catcher with regional flair. Fashioned from delicate crystal flacons, their subdued golden glow illuminates the bar in the evening hours. Modern geometric elements, including the four-part table in the lounge area with its smooth, high-gloss surface and the floor lamp with a lampshade decorated in verdant greenery, underscore the unpretentious character of this first-class design.

A multi-functional bar with regional esprit – a place for business and leisure.

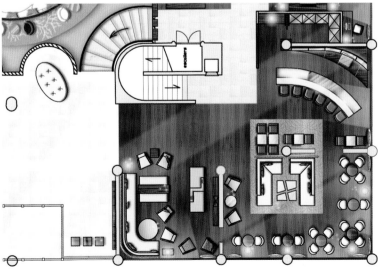

AC Hotel Ambassadeur
Juan-les-Pins, France

Restaurant
Hotel Category: ★ ★ ★ ★ ★
Hotel Type: Resort and conference hotel
Size: 221 rooms
The Brief: Renovation: development of a design concept for the restaurant
Total floor space: Restaurant 182.35 m², Buffet 40.50 m²
Seats: 82

Stimulating and relaxing, authentic and fresh – the design concept for a restaurant with the nous to tick these boxes must evoke an ambience with the power to enchant guests as they start their day with a hearty breakfast bathed in the first rays of sunlight or dine on Mediterranean culinary delights with a glass of wine in pleasant company on a summer's evening.

This light and airy hotel restaurant close to Antibes welcomes guests with an atmosphere that is second to none. Warm, light beige and brown tones define the color scheme, accentuated by green and white elements which tip their hats to the region's famous pine forests. It is a composition which flatters the eye with both elegant restraint and invigoratingly fresh accents. A glass façade floods the restaurant with light, complemented by indirect illumination mounted in large vaulted cornices. In a modern translation, the matt white chandeliers lend the restaurant a stylish and unobtrusive elegance. With its winning interior, the restaurant is the perfect setting for both casual dining and elegant dinners on special occasions.

Restaurant design inspired by pines and French elegance.

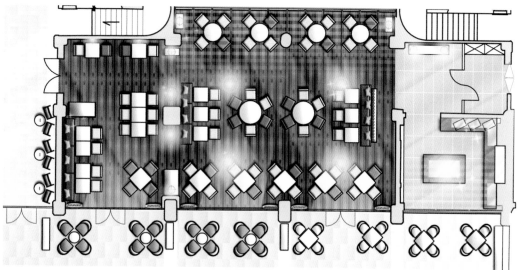

Alpine Views Klosters
Switzerland

Lobby & Bar
Hotel Category: ★ ★ ★ ★ ★
Hotel Type: Resort hotel
Size: 85 rooms
The Brief: New building: development of a design concept for the lobby and bar
Total floor space: Interior 215 m², exterior 120 m²
Seats: Interior 68, exterior 40

What better place could there be to flee the cares of everyday life, revel in tranquility and recharge your batteries than the Alps? The Swiss Alps are an invitation to experience nature in its purest form, whether rambling along mountain trails through forests and flowery meadows in summer, enjoying lunch at a chalet as deer graze in the distance and golden eagles soar above, or zipping down their powdery slopes in winter before retreating inside to the warmth of the fireside. Only the warm embrace of a friend can match the joy of returning comfortably fatigued to one's hotel in the evening to enjoy all the comforts of a first-class facility sporting a design – thankfully bereft of alpine kitsch

– that positively glows in its subscription to Modernity and cosmopolitan esprit.
The reception area and bar offer a modern interpretation of the hotel's natural surroundings that is strong on contrasts and unafraid to dabble with more futuristic elements. The massive and undulating organic form of the white reception counter is reminiscent of a glacier cut by a crevasse. The softer forms are juxtaposed by the massive sculpted bar counter which extends from the reception area through onto the terrace and breaks through the glass façade that separates the exterior zone.

Traditional materiality reinterpreted – a reception area in alpine chic.

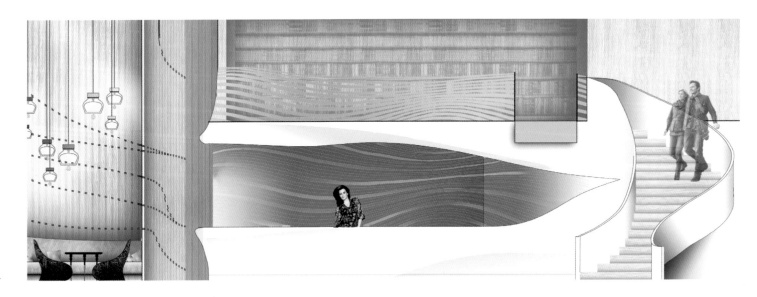

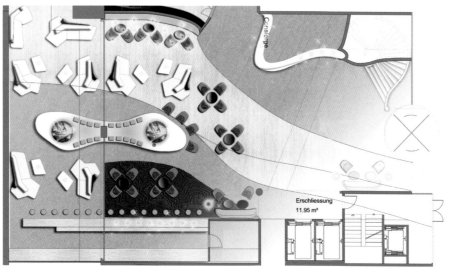

Erschliessung
11.95 m²

Blossom Amsterdam
The Netherlands

Lobby & Bar
Hotel Category: ★ ★ ★ ★ ★
Hotel Type: Boutique hotel
Size: 117 rooms
The Brief: Renovation: development of a design concept for the lobby and bar
Total floor space: Lobby 491 m², bar 124.50 m²
Seats: Lobby 50, bar 31

Amsterdam – the pearl of the Netherlands is a magnet for tourists. The metropolis is a hothouse for the latest fashion and lifestyle designs with a rich cultural landscape that has more to offer than tulips, clogs and Gouda cheese. Take, for example, the world-famous Dutch flower paintings and traditional ceramics.

Set against dark backgrounds and presenting rich shades of yellow and rosé, the color canon of these traditionally sumptuous floral motifs informs this design concept. Entering the lobby, guests are greeted with an artistic floral light installation that literally turns tradition on its head: in a mesmerizing reinterpretation of the traditional reception table, this colorful bouquet appears to sprout from the ceiling, growing down towards the table's round surface. Two angular glass volumes – for the reception and a section of the bar – contrast with the floral elements. The transition to the open-plan bar area is demarcated by the irregular boundary of the parquetry flooring, evoking the soft edges of a petal. The bar's subdued aspect reflects its lounge character and is counterpoised with light, playful details including glass chandeliers and a light sculpture whose white ceramic leaves litter the bar's glass form as if carried there by the wind.

Dutch style – a pleasing combination of traditional and contemporary design.

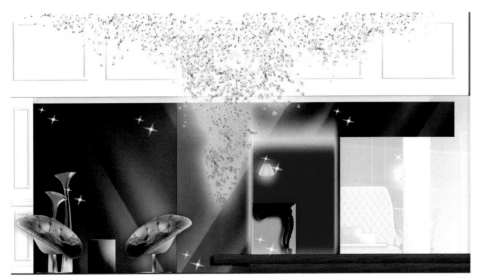

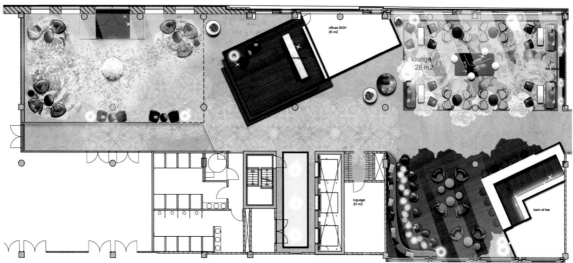

Blossom Amsterdam
The Netherlands

Restaurant
Hotel Category: ★ ★ ★ ★
Hotel Type: Boutique hotel
Size: 117 rooms
The Brief: Renovation: development of a design concept for the restaurant
Total floor space: Restaurant 319.50 m², buffet 38 m²
Seats: Restaurant 126, buffet 8

Ceramics are a traditional material more often than not associated with bulky pots and conventional floor kitchen tiles. But ceramics can do more – from accent features and decorative façade panels through to the most ornate of vases or table lamps, they embody the values of exclusivity and elegance.

The design concept for this restaurant makes full use of ceramics as decorative elements throughout the interior. The light sculpture spanning the length of the ceiling is comprised of ceramic leaves whose various clusters subtly serve to distinguish the restaurant's various zones. Shielding the open kitchen area, ceramic tiles mounted on high-gloss coffered wood panels and decorated with a finely detailed floral pattern strike a pleasing note. Decorated with the same pattern, similar elements have been applied on the side panels of upholstered furnishings. The pattern is inscribed in modified form on the concrete flooring, which forms a cool juxtaposition to its surroundings. A powerful material canon comprising wood, concrete, fine fabrics and ceramics gives rise to an ambience notable for its inventive presentation and blend of classical and modern elements, generating a fresh, vibrant look.

Tradition and elegance – materiality on display.

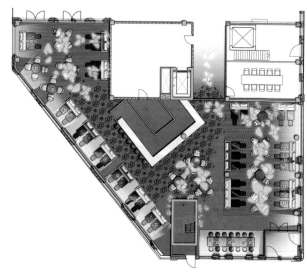

Boutique Hotel Nuremberg
Germany

Lobby / Reception
Hotel Category: ★ ★ ★ ★ superior
Hotel Type: Boutique hotel
Size: 169 rooms
The Brief: Complete redesign: development of a design concept for the reception area
Total floor space: 98.60 m²
Seats: 12

Redesigning an interior within an existing structure can entail considerable challenges – especially in the case of listed architecture – but the opportunity to both enhance and preserve a piece of living history for future generations is often all too rewarding. The younger and young-at-heart Bleisure Generation feel at home in settings that complement vintage elements evocative of times past with an undiluted rendering of contemporary urbanity. This lobby reconciles the old and the new by combining visual designs from across several periods, emphasizing the architectural idiom of the 1930s throughout the interior, enriched with new organic forms and futuristic accents. The result is a young interior with its finger on the pulse of our times that is equally amenable to the demands of guests travelling for leisure, business or – as one does nowadays – bleisure. The somewhat muted color scheme is counterpoised by a selection of materials that are both visually appealing and a pleasure to handle, together with a lighting concept pitched to underscore the dramatic effect of the material scheme.

Turning old into new with urban *bleisure* style.

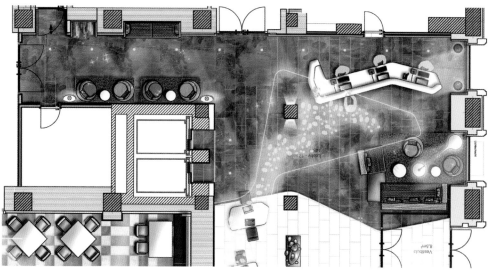

Boutique Hotel Nuremberg
Germany

Bar
Hotel Category: ★ ★ ★ ★ superior
Hotel Type: Boutique hotel
Size: 169 rooms
The Brief: Complete redesign: development of a design concept for the bar
Total floor space: 130.60 m²
Seats: 64

There are countless bars in every city. A few selected among these look back on histories spanning decades – these veterans belong to the bedrock of our cityscapes. Others appear without warning on the back of a new trend and vanish just as abruptly. Creating a unique design concept that is in tune with its times and destined to enjoy more than a fleeting summer of success calls for a precise understanding of what makes a location tick and the style of your target audience. The concept developed for this bar pushes all the right buttons and will appeal to urban day-trippers as well as young business guests with an affinity for quality design. The concept combines contemporary design with personality – the layout is spacious but conveys a sense of intimacy, blending coolness with feel-good elements and a dash of whimsy. The result is at once reserved and sophisticated in its presentation. The design's seemingly disparate qualities complement one another in a visual composition that is intelligent and exciting.

Looking behind the façade – a bar with urban flair.

Boutique Hotel Nuremberg
Germany

Restaurant
Hotel Category: ★ ★ ★ ★ superior
Hotel Type: Boutique hotel
Size: 169 rooms
The Brief: Complete redesign: development of a design concept for the restaurant
Total floor space: Restaurant 181.60 m², buffet 51.70 m²
Seats: 102

Historical architecture frequently evokes associations with ancient and dusty rooms fitted with high-ceilings, decorative stucco elements and massive, ornate furnishings upholstered in the faded brocade of yesterday's splendor. But if you throw all that out the window and create something new that conceals nothing and dares to show a building from its best side, the resulting space will be infused with an atmosphere that is absolutely unique.

This restaurant benefits from the generous height of its ceiling, which is utilized to full effect by a lighting installation spanning its full length. The abstract arrangement of its suspended lighting rods – hanging in the air like Mikado sticks – softens the effect of the generous ceiling height without obscuring its visual strengths. The bright color scheme makes for a breezy atmosphere and the apple green accents of the chairs upholstered in light leather add a breath of fresh air. Lending privacy to the adjoining lounge area, the fuchsia-stained glass wall is a stimulating and eye-catching element which transcends the color canon.

Persuasive without pomp or circumstance – a restaurant in modern urban-chic redux.

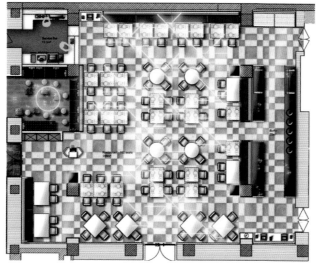

Business Hotel Moscow
Russia

Lobby / Reception
Hotel Category: ★ ★ ★ ★ ★
Hotel Type: Business hotel
Size: 143 rooms
The Brief: New building: development of a design concept for the reception area
Total floor space: 39.20 m²
Seats: 12

When you look at the city map of Moscow, the borders of its various districts look like rings, which represent the growth of the Russian capital in a way similar to the growth rings of a tree trunk. The motif of interwoven rings and ellipses runs through the entire hotel and set-off different hotel areas from each other here as well. Each zone has its own identity and is dedicated to a district of Moscow.

The lobby evokes Red Square with a color scheme that combines red, rust-red and gold. Oval shapes dominate the floor plan causing spatial movement throughout, while a partition uses basic geometric forms as a playful ornamentation which establishes a direct correlation to the traditional patterns of this region. The arc lamps reproduce this leitmotif in the vertical as well, while delineating places of rest. A row of slats draws a fine contrast to these curved shapes and gives a sense of stability. Immersed in a contrast of beige and brown tones, you step up to reception in an elegant ambiance that does not deny its local roots.

Moscow – the city of rings.

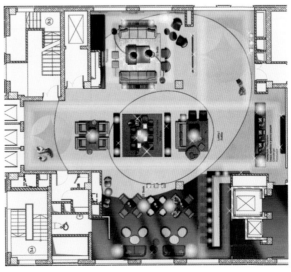

Business Hotel Moscow
Russia

Bar

Hotel Category: ★ ★ ★ ★ ★

Hotel Type: Business hotel

Size: 143 rooms

The Brief: New building: development of a design concept for the bar

Total floor space: 141.40 m²

Seats: 47

The rings of the city are like outward-moving waves that can be felt as far as the bar. They blur the border between the hotel lobby and the bar. Completely isolated areas that are detached from each other are not what international business travelers want today. While zones in a hotel were set more apart from each other in the past, today the transitions between them are more fluid. This is a response to a major change in society today where the difference between work and recreation is increasingly unclear. You can always be reached, can combine fun with work, and you don't always want work to feel like work. Why not check your email while relaxing at the bar with a drink?

Inspiration for the ambience is once again Red Square, but for the bar it's Red Square at night. An interpretation of the many lights that shine there can be found in the wall behind the bar where several rotatable mirrors reflect light in all directions.

A bar like the lights of its city.

28

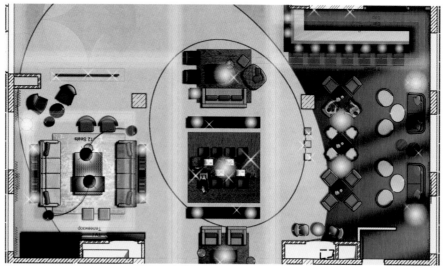

Business Hotel Moscow
Russia

Restaurant
Hotel Category: ★ ★ ★ ★
Hotel Type: Business hotel
Size: 143 rooms
The Brief: New building: development of a design concept for the restaurant
Total floor space: Restaurant 195 m², buffet 20 m²
Seats: 106

Circles and rings are repeated in the hotel-owned restaurant as well. Symbolizing for the different city districts of the Russian capital, the different areas of the restaurant are set-off from each other, each with its own personal feel. Here in the restaurant it's the Boulevard Ring with its parks and public greens that inspires the design. Nature offers a welcome change of atmosphere during a break between meetings. Here you can refuel, take a deep breath and get ready for whatever you have to face. The design interpretation for the interior of the restaurant is conveyed by a row of semi-transparent suspended lamps made of wood, a material meant to evoke trees in a Moscow park. Their spherical shape firmly integrates them into the overall design concept and also provides a sense of stability to the tables below. A poetical interpretation of the design theme here can be found in the glasses and bottles cupboard behind the bar, where leaf motifs in fine copper wire seem to rise through the room on a gust of wind.

Using nature to artistically configure a restaurant.

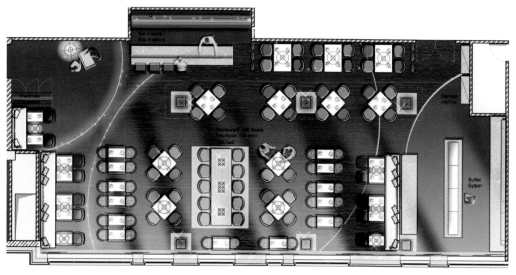

Cruiser

Lobby
Category: ★ ★ ★ ★ ★ superior
Type: Luxury yacht
Size: 132 cabins
The Brief: New building: development of a design concept for the lobby
Total floor space: 132.60 m²
Seats: 10

At a fundamental level, the worlds of hospitality and yacht design are not dissimilar. Here too, luxury, exclusivity, uniqueness and individuality are the core values – especially in the premium segment. For instance on the awe-inspiring super yachts that sail the seven seas to weigh anchor at some of the world's most beautiful harbors and idyllic beaches.

Who hasn't dreamt of escaping to a deserted and untouched beach, tucked away in a secluded bay, its turquoise waters disturbed only by the anchor's splash as it slips below the surface on what promises to be an unforgettable summer's day? A glass of champagne, sir? Canapés, madam? Life can be oh-so sweet – as the interior design of this luxury yacht shows all too well. A

canon of exquisite materials, including light marble and warm rosewood surfaces, sets the mood: dressed in composite material, three individual reception units welcome guests aboard with the necessary decorum and discretion, their structured surfaces evocative of the undulating touch of ocean waves on sand. The ornate coral forms of the table lamps decorating the reception units set striking accents. Like air bubbles rising to the water's surface, a lighting sculpture comprised of glass spheres completes the design – a reminiscence of the luxury yacht's natural element.

Welcome aboard the luxury yacht: life is sweet.

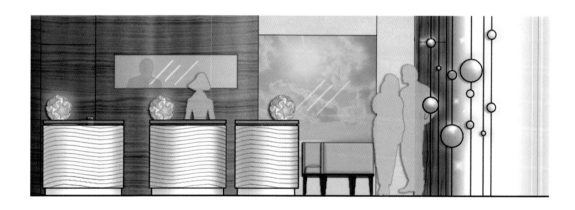

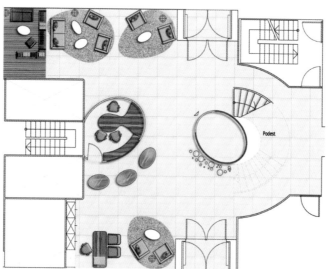

Podest

Cruiser

Restaurant

Category: ★ ★ ★ ★ ★ superior

Type: Luxury yacht

Size: 132 cabins

The Brief: New building: development of a design concept for the restaurant

Total floor space: 233.70 m²

Seats: 111

Whatever the similarities in the aesthetics of hotels and super yachts, creating successful interior designs for these ocean vessels requires a heightened sensibility and deep understanding of the demands of the maritime environment. Knowing which materials cope best in these conditions and how they can be protected is key. It would be a tragedy if the marble surfaces, fine woods and exquisite fabrics of these floating wonders lost their luster within weeks. Besides the actual design itself, resilience and safety play an equally important role in the development of the material canon. The private atmosphere of this exclusive restaurant is created through the spacious zoning of the individual seating islands.

Natural colors and a blend of high-quality leather surfaces upholstered fabrics, stone, glass and a variety of timbers makes for a haptic experience notable for its contrasts. The quality of these materials speaks for itself, rendering superfluous the use of more scintillating elements. Glass wall panels with coral motifs segment the space without diminishing its spaciousness. The centerpiece: a high table flanked by bar stools is the ideal place to meet with fellow passengers and wax lyrical about the highlights of the previous days over a glass of wine.

Anchors aweigh – a restaurant for pure luxury and indulgence.

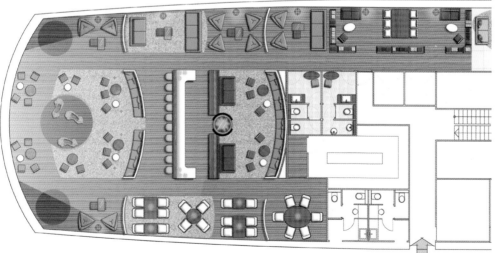

Diamond Tower Berlin
Germany

Lobby	
Hotel Category:	★ ★ ★ ★ ★ luxury
Hotel Type:	City hotel
Size:	232 rooms
The Brief:	New building: development of a design concept for the lobby
Total floor space:	327.20 m²
Seats:	15

Materials of the highest quality, hand-crafted individual pieces, exclusive and glamorous design – this is luxury in its most unadulterated form. The stunning look of the flooring, wall surfaces and furniture speaks for itself. Guests will be won over entirely by this design when they discover that it is as pleasing to the touch as it is to the eye. The finish is first-class throughout, right down to the smallest seam.

Dazzling expressions of luxury, diamonds epitomize the spirit of this five-star hotel in the heart of Berlin – the highlight in contemporary premium hospitality in this glamorous city. In the same way that a connoisseur delights in the discovery of a rare piece of flawless glassware, guests will be enchanted by this lobby. The glittering centerpiece of this breathtaking space: the diamond forms of the floating light sculptures, seemingly fashioned from thousands of smaller precious stones. The master craftsmanship apparent in the polished finish of these diamonds is underscored by the dazzling rays of the accent lines, which cut across the black surface of the lobby's natural stone floor in a dramatic flourish. The light coloration and fine tufted leather upholstery of the columns forms a soft counterpoint to the cool elegance of this dazzling visual performance.

A crystalline design vocabulary and materiality: impressive, appealing, fascinating.

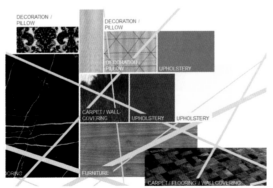

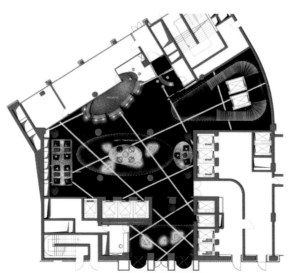

Diamond Tower Berlin
Germany

Restaurant
Hotel Category: ★ ★ ★ ★ ★ luxury
Hotel Type: City hotel
Size: 232 rooms
The Brief: New building: development of a design concept for the restaurant
Total floor space: Restaurant 537.20 m², buffet 49.30 m²
Seats: 202

If the reception area sets the standard with its breathtaking look and abundance of high-end material, the restaurant takes excellence one step further, ensuring that guests will not be disappointed. The gourmet restaurant of this luxury hotel can hold its head high: its glitzy design is sure to impress and invites guests to take their seats at tables lovingly arranged with the greatest care and attention to detail. Crystal moments: eye-catching chandeliers evoke the ambience of a ballroom, but it is the masterpiece shielding the buffet that steals the show with a form reminiscent of a precision cut gemstone. The golden shimmer of its glass surface catches the light, lending the restaurant a warm glow and concealing the buffet zone in the most charming fashion imaginable. The glamorous atmosphere is accentuated by the opulent Baroque patterning of the upholstery and wall coverings, complemented by modern furniture to ensure the look is light and contemporary. Surrounded by dazzling crystals, fine fabrics and precious natural stones and woods, guests could retreat into the luxurious ambience of this world of elegance for hours or even days on end...

Beauty in perfection – an interior design fascinated by crystals.

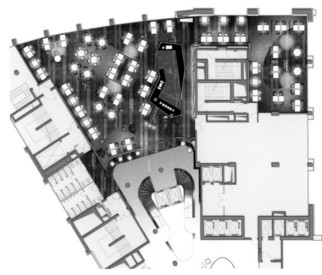

Dolce Munich Unterschleißheim
Germany

Lobby
Hotel Category: ★ ★ ★ ★
Hotel Type: Conference hotel
Size: 255 rooms
The Brief: New building: development of a design concept for the lobby
Total floor space: 390 m²
Seats: 27

The capacity to emphasize regional identity in design without falling into cliché is an art in itself. The designer's passion for local color must be tempered by strict adherence to the highest standards of quality – only the best of materials will suffice. However, fitting it might seem at first glance, a single design element that fails to make the grade can undermine an entire presentation rather than infusing it with authenticity.

At this hotel situated in the south of Germany, the interior skillfully bridges the divide between Bavarian tradition and contemporary lifestyle. The hotel wears its regional loyalty on its sleeve: stylized cow bells in honey-tinted oak adorn the violet wall backing the reception. Hunting trophies and artfully arranged *Dirndl* and *Lederhosen* decorate the public areas, ensuring that neither domestic nor international guests will forget where they happen to be for even the briefest of moments. These playful visual references to Bavarian culture charm the eye and are carefully incorporated within the overall design concept.

Check in with the feel-good ambience of Bavaria.

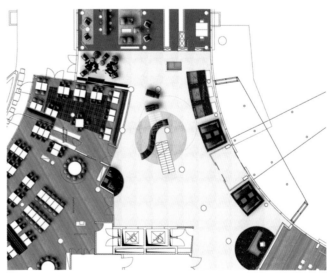

Dolce Munich Unterschleißheim
Germany

Bar
Hotel Category: ★ ★ ★ ★
Hotel Type: Conference hotel
Size: 255 rooms
The Brief: New building: development of a design concept for the bar
Total floor space: 209 m²
Seats: 73

Authenticity is often inseparably linked with natural appeal. Colors and materials – a destination Made by Nature. The material canon utilized here is subtle and exclusive, comprising native timbers, bronzed metal, polished concrete, leather, loden and cowhide.

Linking directly to the reception area, this spacious lounge bar presents a sophisticated vision of the mountain chalet. A calm, neutral spectrum of colors reflects the values of the Bavarian landscape, broken only by individual color accents such as the raspberry violet table. The cowhide upholstery of the tubular steel armchairs invites guests to take time out, while a scattering of hides about the room cuts an impressive figure. An open fireplace featuring a natural stonework mosaic is framed by cross-sections of timber. Natural materials including oak, slate, stone and metal predominate and exude an aura of luxury. Setting modern accents, several of the massive oak stools are dressed in white lacquer. An open-plan design with a long table flanked by small groups of chairs encourages communication – a welcoming setting for leisure and business guests.

Zeitgeist, **lifestyle and regional authenticity – Bavarian hospitality 2.0.**

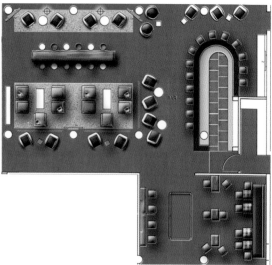

Dolce Munich Unterschleißheim
Germany

Restaurant / Fine Dining
Hotel Category: ★ ★ ★ ★
Hotel Type: Conference hotel
Size: 255 rooms
The Brief: New building: development of a design concept for the fine dining restaurant 'Redox'
Total floor space: 72 m²
Seats: 40
Finalist: European Hotel Design Awards 2010
Adex Platinum Award 2011

With a warm and welcoming interior that encourages communication and leaves space for inspiration to flourish, this hotel hits all the right notes. Our design evokes an atmosphere that will seduce guests, tempting them to stay longer or, at the very least to return. The restaurant is a key element within a design concept that is especially sophisticated for an interior of this kind.

The overarching theme of this interior design – regional authenticity – looms large here, heightening the gourmet restaurant's ambience of exclusivity, style and individuality with subtle nods to Bavarian culture. In keeping with this aspiration, the interior presents a modern interpretation of traditional values, combining rectilinear structures with regional references and ingenious details – not infrequently with a wry sense of humor. The softwood wall paneling is reminiscent of traditional country inns, empty picture frames let the imagination run wild, and the intelligent application of lighting effects – including chandeliers crafted from antlers – sets additional accents.

Earthy, elegant, elementary: fine dining in a Bavarian idyll.

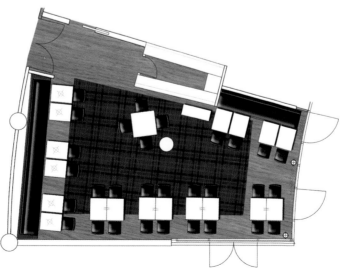

DoubleTree by Hilton Oradea
Romania

Lobby / Reception
Hotel Category: ★ ★ ★ ★
Hotel Type: Business hotel
Size: 154 rooms
The Brief: New building: development of a design concept for the reception area
Total floor space: 226.55 m²
Seats: 22

This hotel is situated on a lowland plain surrounded by the Apuseni Mountains of Romania. In a location shaped by the forces of history and nature, the hotel combines cosmopolitan chic with a sensitive awareness of regional design values. The hotel is well-placed to satisfy the needs of business guests, day-trippers and residents celebrating special occasions.

In a visual reference to Oradea's thousand-year-old fortress, the pentagonal outline of its ground plan figures in the flooring, ceiling mounted cove lights and side tables in the lobby. The hotel's reception area is distinguished by the playful character of its materiality: finished in warm walnut, the reception desk adds depth to the space with a mirror mounted on the side facing into the lobby – its surface is illuminated indirectly with LED strip lights and partially concealed by a curtain of vertically arranged pearl chains crafted in metal. Decorated with a grid-like arrangement of metal pilaster strips and finished in black high-gloss lacquer, the paneled wall surfaces behind the desk lend the reception area a formal frame and exert a calming influence.

The pearl of Oradea: a hotel on the Crișul Repede River.

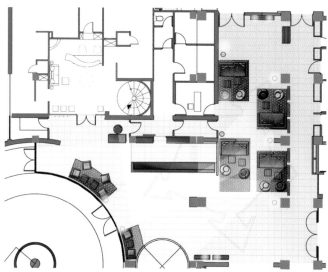

DoubleTree by Hilton Oradea
Romania

Bar
Hotel Category: ★ ★ ★ ★
Hotel Type: Business hotel
Size: 154 rooms
The Brief: New building: development of a design concept for the bar
Total floor space: 121.30 m²
Seats: 56

Once the haunt of Count Dracula, Oradea and the surrounding region are shrouded in an aura of mysticism. At a level that is perhaps barely perceptible to guests, this history is reflected in the color canon and formal vocabulary informing the design concept of this bar.

Contrasts abound as chandeliers and opulently gilded picture frames meet with the clean vocabulary of the modern suspended light fittings and rounded forms of the chairs and armchairs. Reconciling the contemporary with the cozy, the lively atmosphere at the bar is complemented by a peaceful lounge area. Drapes are on hand if required to close off the glass façade looking out over the river and create a more intimate space for guests seated nearby. A fireplace in the lounge makes for a homely atmosphere and adds warmth. A carpet defines this space – patterned with the geometric vertices seen in the chandeliers – setting it off from the remainder of the bar, which is laid out with refined wood flooring.

An aura of mysticism – contrasts abound in this design.

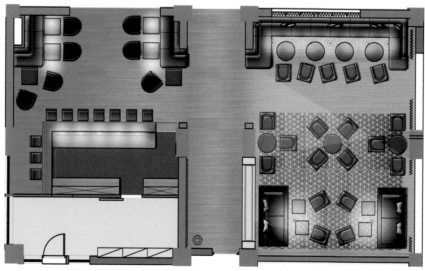

Eye of Black Sea Odessa
Ukraine

Lobby / Reception
Hotel Category: ★ ★ ★ ★ ★ luxury
Hotel Type: Resort and business hotel
Size: 285 rooms
The Brief: New building: development of a design concept for the reception area
Total floor space: 300.20 m²
Seats: 24

An impressive construction project directly on the seafront – one of Odessa's most beautiful features. The building extends on stilts into the Black Sea. Guests can hardly get closer to the water. It quickly became clear that water must play a major role in the interior design of this luxury hotel in a special setting. It permeates every area, sometimes boldly, sometimes gently. It can be visible at first glance, or merely sensed. As the hotel's introduction, the entrance immediately presents several facets of the theme. Wayfinding and initial orientation are most important. Where am I? How do I move in this space? A gentle, irregular wave in the form of strips set flush in the floor guides me into the building interior, the elevators, and even further, back out again to the bar and terrace. Individual desks for personal reception shaped like shells or pebbles on the beach are positioned on one side in front of a wood slat background resembling sea grass bent by the wind. A finely tuned lighting concept highlights the backdrop with further accents.

A reception area under the water sign.

Eye of Black Sea Odessa
Ukraine

Lobby Bar

Hotel Category: ★ ★ ★ ★ ★ luxury
Hotel Type: Resort and business hotel
Size: 285 rooms
The Brief: New building: development of a design concept for the lobby bar
Total floor space: Interior 218.40 m², exterior 299.50 m²
Seats: Interior 77, exterior 125

In a seafront setting such as this, it's only natural that everything takes its cue from the view of the cool waters. The lobby bar, which adjoins the hotel entrance, offers more outdoor than indoor seats, because in fine weather guests naturally sit at the water's edge. Especially since the building extends out over the water, so guests are on the same plane as the fish. Curving slat assemblies that function as a backdrop on the surrounding walls indicate the connection to reception. In front is a bar, where all seating is oriented toward the water. The same holds for the long banquette in front.

A clearly arranged room completely oriented toward the view.
And the interior mirrors the outdoors. The interior design plays with references to the marine world, holding to natural tones paired with fresh accents in light green. The centerpiece is a sea of irregular glass globes, like underwater air bubbles, that lets guests plunge deep into this other world.

A bar with vision.

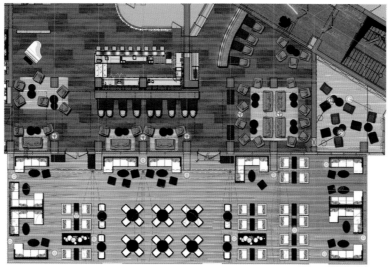

Eye of Black Sea Odessa
Ukraine

Sky Bar
Hotel Category: ★ ★ ★ ★ ★ luxury
Hotel Type: Resort and business hotel
Size: 285 rooms
The Brief: New building: development of a design concept for the Sky Bar
Total floor space: 307.95 m²
Seats: 120

There is another, very different bar on the upper floors of the hotel tower. With a view of the beautiful Black Sea coast and the certainty of a breathtaking sunset, a visit to the Sky Bar provides a further highlight for night owls during their stay. Business meetings come to a sociable conclusion or a day at the beach comes to an exhilarating end among people after an entire day spent with the family. Cool drinks and a high-spirited turn on the dance floor are included.

Backlit columns distinguish the interior and the gleaming white, organically shaped bar offers interaction. Glasses on the bar leave traces and mark the guest's place. The bar is set in a curved lighting installation that winds through the room like its formal inspiration, the pulsating waves beyond the windows. The light pulses in time with the music and the color changes with its pitch. This light show can also be seen from the front of the building, inviting a visit.

A search for traces – the interactive bar.

Eye of Black Sea Odessa
Ukraine

Cigar Lounge
Hotel Category: ★ ★ ★ ★ ★ luxury
Hotel Type: Resort and business hotel
Size: 285 rooms
The Brief: New building: development of a design concept for the cigar lounge
Total floor space: 85.20 m²
Seats: 38

Someone who prefers to retire with a cigar in the evening, but does not wish to forego the impressive sea view from the upper floors of the hotel tower, will find a seat in the cigar lounge immediately adjacent to the Sky Bar. After a few dances in the adjoining club or simply for relaxation after a strenuous day; the view from up here is unique and unquestionably worth seeing on every visit!

The interior? It is subdued and frames the view of the evening sky. Interplay of different brown shades, from Havana to cognac, from coffee to caramel. Everything the heart desires in a sophisticated end to the day. Seating alcoves, wing chairs, books and humidors define the atmosphere. The ambience is one of subdued finery opened up by special lighting effects in gold and high quality custom carpeting in the same shades. The windows frame the view to the outside, each one crowned highlighted by a specially created chandelier.

Eye of Black Sea – the name says it all.

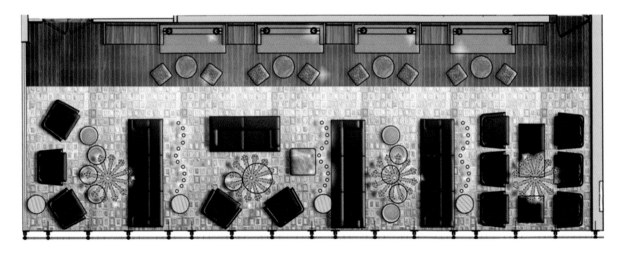

Fleet Side Hamburg
Germany

Lobby / Bar
Hotel Category: ★ ★ ★ ★ superior
Hotel Type: City hotel
Size: 225 rooms
The Brief: Renovation: development of a design concept for the lobby with bar
Total floor space: 246.50 m²
Seats: 62

Every city has its symbols and attractions that are characteristic for its identity – from distinctive works of architecture, to natural environments and traces of history in the cityscape. Regional customs and traditions add their own particular color to our urban environments. Creating an authentic design concept is all about identifying these elements and calibrating their role within the finished product. Elements of local color are often only apparent at a second (or third...) glance – even to the locals... and yet they can make or break a hotel's atmosphere and wider appeal.

This concept for Bricks Hamburg toys with a range of motifs including the city's port, the nearby waterfront, warehouses and the Alster – a mix of the rustic and the refined in which Hamburg's salt of-the-earth spirit takes on a sophisticated bend. Exquisite dark woods set the tone in the lobby with its open bar area, complemented by classy leather surfaces in beige and fetching upholstered furniture dressed in warm browns and reds. To the rear of the bar sits a long high table flanked by bar stools and a massive shelving unit laden with seductive spices, coffee beans and teas from Hamburg's port and Speicherstadt warehouses.

Local color done right. Check in and experience the best of Hamburg.

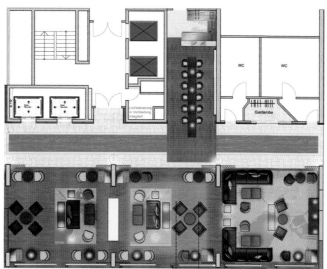

Fleet Side Hamburg
Germany

Restaurant
Hotel Category: ★ ★ ★ ★ superior
Hotel Type: City hotel
Size: 225 rooms
The Brief: Renovation: development of a design concept for the restaurant
Total floor space: Restaurant 322 m²; buffet 85.50 m²
Seats: 172

From the very first moment that a guest steps through the door, their experience will be defined by a hotel's design concept. Taking its visual cues from the city of Hamburg, this design concept offers a different perspective at every turn. In the lobby, the influence of Hamburg's port and Speicherstadt warehouse district are readily apparent in an interpretation that is rustic yet refined. Approaching the restaurant, Hamburg's Alster waterways take center-stage as the interior assumes a decidedly elegant and sophisticated flavor.

At the heart of the restaurant: the main bar – framed by free-standing columns dressed in cor-ten steel with its distinctive rust patina. The individually welded and riveted panels are reminiscent of a ship's hull and bring a hint of maritime flair into the heart of the hotel. Two recesses feature tailor-made wine racks in which bottles of red wine chill in an eye-catching backlit display. Mirrors mounted in picture frames line the restaurant's walls. Catching the sun, their glittering surfaces evoke the shimmering waters of Hamburg's Alster lakes. A contoured ceiling in hues of white and gray heightens the vibrant spirit of this restaurant.

Take a seat and relax. A restaurant like a boat trip on Hamburg's Alster.

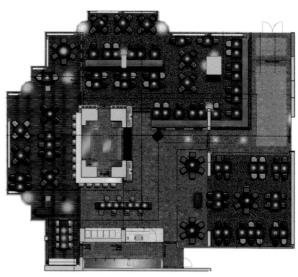

Four Points by Sheraton Zaporozhye, Ukraine

Lobby

Hotel Category: ★ ★ ★ ★

Hotel Type: Business hotel

Size: 164 rooms

The Brief: New building: development of a design concept for the lobby

Total floor space: 408.90 m²

Seats: 40

Zaporozhye – this historically important industrial center and transportation hub has made a name for itself in recent years as a quirky cultural metropolis. The creation of a coherent design concept calls for the rare talent to recognize a location's inner character and tap into its history – the design for this hotel in the Ukraine is a textbook example. The idea: to create a concept rich in natural appeal, with plenty of high quality timber and warm colors in a modern translation of traditional designs.

Just how well these qualities combine is readily apparent to guests from the moment they set foot in the lobby. The Ukraine's new national symbol – the sunflower – greets guests from the ceiling. A cloud of colored glass spheres comprising an abstract vision of the classical chandelier infuses the space with light. Its radiant form is reflected and complemented in the crème white accents decorating the beige marble floor below, heightening its visual impact. But it is the curving double staircase with its elegant flights of illuminated marble steps that steals the show. The stylish reception desk with its radiant counter shows how well the Ukraine's traditional colors – blue and yellow – translate into a modern composition that is more than pleasing to the eye.

Modern elegance with natural appeal – a lobby like a sunflower in bloom.

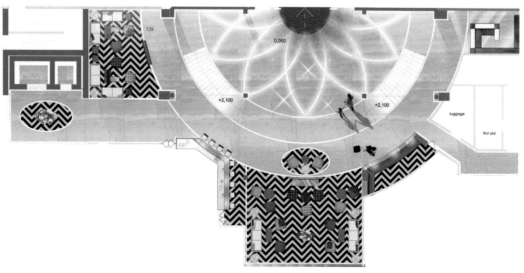

Four Points by Sheraton Zaporozhye, Ukraine

Bar
Hotel Category: ★ ★ ★ ★
Hotel Type: Business hotel
Size: 164 rooms
The Brief: New building: development of a design concept for the bar
Total floor space: 287.60 m²
Seats: 53

The digital age is one of rapid change and immersive technology. We are always online and always available. Design details that capture a sense of authenticity can evoke warm memories of times past, giving us pause for thought – if only for a moment. Viewed in isolation, seemingly vintage and antique objects may seem old-fashioned, but in combination with a modern form vocabulary and materials they take us to previously unknown heights of comfort and homeliness.

This bar encompasses an additional two areas, delimited by the herringbone patterning of the flooring. Located just a few steps away, these quieter areas are ideal for conducting business in a stylish ambience.

The utilization of vintage design elements throughout the bar makes for a homely atmosphere. Dark brown leather armchairs and sofas populate the bar, decorated with a sprinkling of scatter cushions in shades of turquoise. The panels sheathing the bar are reminiscent of amber in its natural state – raw and unpolished – their earthy quality lends nature a presence within this space. The delicate sculptural installation positioned to its side – a veil of glass spheres – evokes an air of ease and elegance, fascinating guests as its globes catch the sun like bubbles and refract its rays.

A space for business and pleasure – a modern bar and lounge with vintage elements.

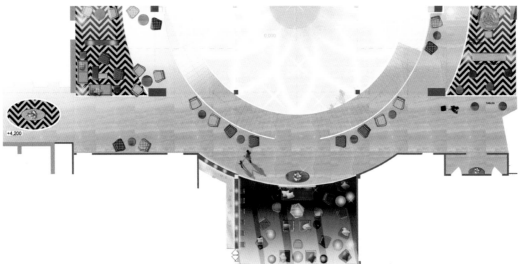

Golf Resort Belek
Turkey

Reception and Public Areas
Hotel Category: ★ ★ ★ ★ ★ luxury
Hotel Type: Resort hotel
Size: 230 rooms
The Brief: New building: development of a design concept for the reception and public areas
Total floor space: 2,337 m²
Seats: Lobby 170

A hotel project in a class of its own. A facility with main building, private villas, two premium golf courses and all the recreational activities you could wish for. An attractive luxury spa, four different pool areas, food and fun is everywhere – from rustic and typical Turkish bars, to private gourmet restaurants, to nightclubs under open skies, even something for the kids. In fact, children are well looked-after at a supervised location somewhat hidden from the activities around the main building. This gives parents time for themselves, lets them kick back and relax for a change.

The reception area in the main building combines several functions on one floor. It is a large entrance hall with fountains and an inner courtyard, a lobby, bar, restaurants, along with a banquet area, conference rooms, a day spa, hair salon and bazaar – everything comes together here. The floor plan is a labyrinth whose surface area is structured by a strict symmetry. This makes it easy to find your way and it inspires you to discover new things, all in an ambiance that combines the oriental and the modern. Because as a tourist, you want to feel the traditional character of the place you're visiting, yet still enjoy all the amenities of the present.

The Ottoman Empire meets the future – a new interpretation of the luxury hotel.

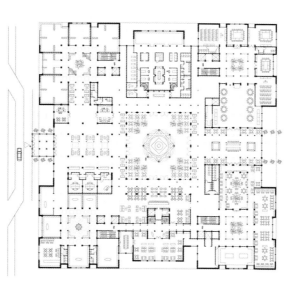

Hafenlodge Hamburg
Germany

Restaurant Lounge
Category: Upscale
Type: Business clientele
The Brief: New building: development of a design concept for the restaurant lounge
Total floor space: Interior 107.90 m², exterior 64.80 m²
Seats: Interior 45, exterior 28

Where's the best place to experience Hamburg and the city's history? On the River Elbe, of course, at the harbor. One can smell the sea here, a breeze from the big, wide world. A special side of the city; this is where longings are awakened, where rugged seafaring meets today's metropolis. A colorful mixture of cultures. A seductive ambience. For centuries rugs from all over the world, spices, coffee and tea have been traded here and then shipped to foreign lands. This lounge in the new office district, overlooking the hustle and bustle, reflects the local coloration and transposes it into a contemporary design language.

Slats that do not block the view, an abstract Japanese koi fish on the ceiling, herringbone parquet on the floor, white lamps dancing like foam in the harbor basin and a kitchen line with fronts tilted like the surface of water in the wind. They encourage communication: visitors can cook together here, dine at the long table and then move to more relaxed, upholstered seating in the lounge or on the terrace.

The harbor's colors – captured in contemporary design.

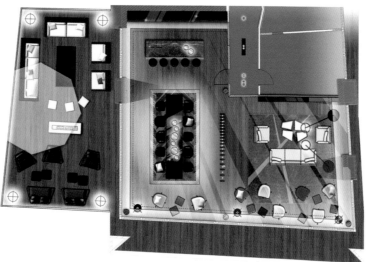

Hilton Vienna Danube
Austria

Lobby

Hotel Category: ★ ★ ★ ★ superior
Hotel Type: Business hotel
Size: 367 rooms
The Brief: Complete renovation: development of a design concept for the lobby
Total floor space: 388.90 m²
Seats: 30
Architect: Christian Heiss

The Danube and Vienna are in the heart of Europe. For hundreds of years, this former imperial capital and residence of the Habsburg dynasty was seen as the most important urban center on the Danube, which today it shares with several other major European cities. Located directly on the river bank, the hotel offers a magical view of this beautiful body of water.

No other city has been as successful as Vienna for so long at unifying contrasts and giving them a distinct character, which is visible everywhere in the city's historical buildings. Built in 1912, the hotel was a granary before it was transformed into a hotel in the mid-1980s. Only the wide pillars in the lobby indicate the original purpose of the structure. However, these pillars are barely noticeable, because when you enter the large, two-story foyer your field of vision is automatically drawn in a straight line over the carpet – in pleasantly dark colors with red stripes and curving ornamentation – to the large window at the back. This gives visitors their first chance to experience the hotel's unique view of the Danube. To offset the size of the lobby, a collection of several suspended lamps, round and made of glass, are installed at different heights. Their round shapes form a nice contrast to the square pillar shapes.

Traditional yet modern, metropolitan yet cozy – Viennese charm at its best.

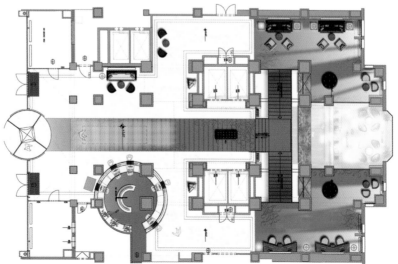

Hilton Vienna Danube
Austria

Bar

Hotel Category: ★ ★ ★ ★ superior
Hotel Type: Business hotel
Size: 367 rooms
The Brief: Complete renovation: development of a design concept for the bar
Total floor space: 240.40 m²
Seats: 57
Architect: Christian Heiss

The unique location is the basis for everything here. In renovating this hotel, everything focused on providing an open view of the Danube, and on using the motifs of moving waves and water throughout the entire design concept.

Passing through the lobby, you'll find a stairway leading down a story to the bar, which is actually located on the ground floor at river level. This modern bar's many lighting elements make it glow like the Vienna Prater amusement park. Besides the bar itself with backlighting, another real eye-catcher here is the area near the stairs with a wall of green, orange and yellow lights. These bring color to the

design composition, while the body of the bar – made of high-quality natural stone – contributes genuine, natural warmth. The lounge area of the bar, on the other hand, has subdued lighting combined with comfortable furniture in soft grey and brown tones for a cozy atmosphere. For relaxing there is the modern interpretation of the classic winged easy chair where you can watch the fire crackling in the fireplace. These set-off this space from the rest of the bar and give you an open view of the areas behind.

Waves on the Danube rather than a piece of Sachertorte – a river as design inspiration.

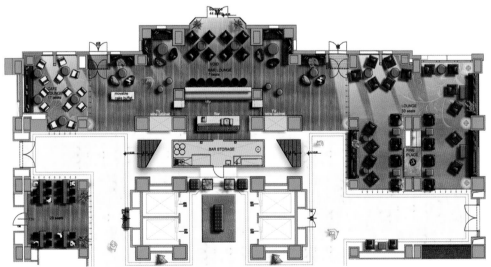

Hilton Frankfurt Airport 'THE SQUAIRE', Germany

Lobby

Hotel Category: ★ ★ ★ ★ ★
Hotel Type: Luxury business hotel
Size: 249 rooms
The Brief: New building: development of a design concept for the lobby
Total floor space: 521.20 m²
Seats: 22

Top hotel opening award 2011 – category 'luxury'
International Hotel Awards 2012 / 2013: Best New Hotel Construction & Design Germany
Finalist: European Hotel Design Awards 2012

THE SQUAIRE at Frankfurt Airport is a building project of superlatives. One side of the 600-meter long structure is on stilts above the ICE high-speed train line, surrounded by autobahns and right next to one of Europe's largest airports – the other side borders on the pristine natural surroundings of the Stadtwald Forest. From far away, this building expresses the dynamics of travel and mobility, which is also carried forth on the inside where tired travelers nonetheless find a haven where they can slow down and relax.

The combination of movement and repose can be experienced and felt as soon as you enter the hotel. The huge lobby's high ceiling is lowered to a homier, cozier level by two golden roof elements that spread out like wings on the left and right. They make it feel like you've had a soft landing, you've arrived. And now you can relax in a sheltered atmosphere. The reception area also unifies contrasts – cubes made of satin-finished stainless steel framed in painted glass are integrated into the organic form of a counter structure made of leather and dark, smoked oak. Eye-catchers here are the small, pole-mounted lamps made of polished aluminum. Articulated by round, curved lines they are a small reminder of the exterior design of the building.

The 'immobility of mobility' – unifying the dynamics of travel with rest and comfort.

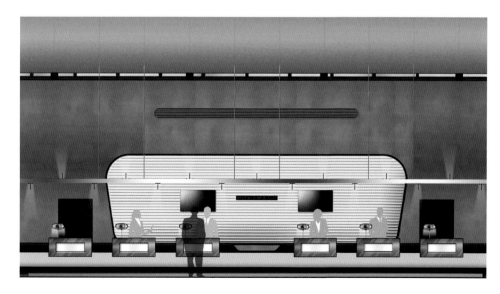

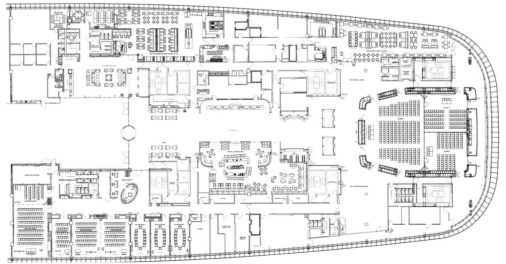

Hilton Frankfurt Airport 'THE SQUAIRE', Germany

Bar

Hotel Category: ★ ★ ★ ★ ★
Hotel Type: Luxury business hotel
Size: 249 rooms
The Brief: New building: development of a design concept for 'THE FIFTH Lounge & Bar'
Total floor space: 284.90 m²
Seats: 122

Top hotel opening award 2011 – category 'luxury'
International Hotel Awards 2012 / 2013: Best New Hotel Construction & Design Germany
Finalist: European Hotel Design Awards 2012

Most important for discerning business travelers when choosing a hotel are good connections to all means of transportation, technological equipment and comfort – in both the room and the hotel's public areas. Winding-down after a long trip or endless meetings is a top priority, if you're going to be fresh and rested the next day, which can be just as long.

Opposite the reception is THE FIFTH Lounge & Bar offering hotel guests a great place to relax in a cozy atmosphere after checking in. In the evening it's the perfect place for a drink after work or for a glass of wine with friends. The warm, natural colors of the furniture here combine with the floral wallpaper for a calm flair. Look closely and you'll see finely illuminated movement in the bar counter made of 3D-formed composite material – a reference to the futuristic façade of the building – and in the wall paneling of thin ribs.

Arrive, take a deep breath and relax – a bar for business travelers to wind down in.

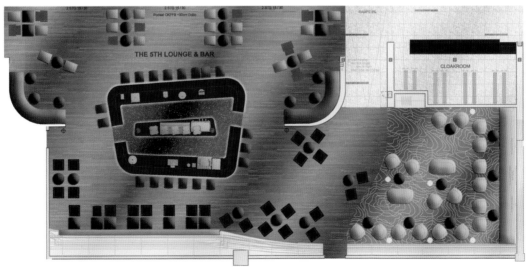

THE 5TH LOUNGE & BAR

CLOAKROOM

Hilton Frankfurt Airport 'THE SQUAIRE', Germany

Executive Lounge
Hotel Category: ★ ★ ★ ★ ★
Hotel Type: Luxury business hotel
Size: 249 rooms
The Brief: New building: development of a design concept for renovating the Executive Lounge
Total floor space: Executive Lounge 287.10 m², buffet 28 m²
Seats: 82
Top hotel opening award 2011 – category 'luxury'
International Hotel Awards 2012 / 2013: Best New Hotel Construction & Design Germany
Finalist: European Hotel Design Awards 2012

Comfort at its best that's still able to meet all the needs of business travelers – at one location tailor-made to their exact requirements. This was the objective of designing the Executive Lounge.

The computers can be lowered out of sight into the large reception tables whose high-quality, dark brown surfaces made of walnut form an ideal contrast to the dynamic movement of the light, rib-like fronts – again in homage to the dynamic outer design of the building. In contrast to this is the warm cocooning effect created by the freestanding seat niches made of light-colored leather. Here you can work undisturbed and shielded from prying eyes. Of course, you can also use the room as a lounge to kick-back in, or to relax in a comfortable leather easy chair while waiting on a delayed flight. And if your flight takes off early in the morning, the hotel offers an early-bird breakfast in the adjacent buffet area where glowing pink lamps help drive away fatigue and refresh you with their soft, pleasant light.

Business travel at its very best – the Executive Lounge.

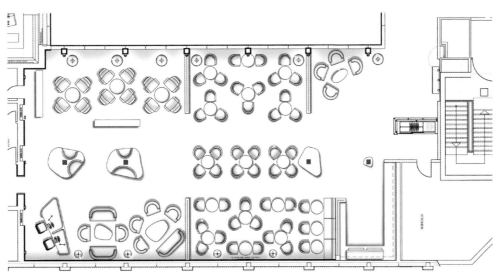

Hilton Munich Park
Germany

Lobby

Hotel Category: ★ ★ ★ ★

Hotel Type: Business hotel

Size: 484 rooms

The Brief: Complete renovation: development of a design concept for the lobby

Total floor space: 676.90 m²

Seats: 98

Finalist: European Hospitality Award 2012

Located in the Bavarian capital's famed English Garden and with the ever-popular Eisbach stream at its doorstep, the hotel borders Munich's green lung. The design is inspired by the hotel's natural surroundings, with a wealth of details that explore this theme in a modern translation.

Dressed in warm, earthen tones with accents in gray and golden yellow, the capacious oval form of the lobby brings the park into the interior while creating a private atmosphere. Balustrades reinterpret the classical garden hedgerow, shielding and holding guests in their embrace, with a range of seating elements of various heights inviting guests to linger. A sofa describes a gentle S-curve for those on more intimate terms, while to the side bar stools provide a casual staging area for brief conversations and 'Early Bird' breakfasts as guests hurry to the airport. A light sculpture made from transparent petals trails from the ceiling, lending further emphasis to this area. In the background, the clear and dynamic lines of a lighting installation framing the reception desks break with the space's organic vocabulary of form and build a bridge to the present day.

Take a walk in the park: natural beauty in a modern translation.

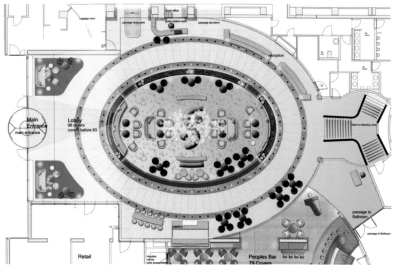

Hilton Munich Park
Germany

Bar

Hotel Category: ★ ★ ★ ★ ★
Hotel Type: Business hotel
Size: 484 rooms
The Brief: Complete renovation: development of a design concept for the 'People's Bar'
Total floor space: 146.80 m²
Seats: 39
Finalist: European Hospitality Award 2012

A journey into beauty: careful exploration of the natural forms, colors and structures to be found at a site as beautiful as Munich's English Garden will turn up inspiration for countless interpretations that can be incorporated into hotel interiors. The park is a tangible presence throughout this hotel – balustrades inspired by garden thickets and hedgerows shield the bar from the lobby. Within, floral patterns adorn the flooring and walls, electrified by the scintillating fine lines of a design concept inspired by nature. Light effects underscore this playful translation of natural forms, together with a combination of materials selected to add the necessary degree of decorum and glamour, and a dialog of soft, deep pile textiles with metallic surfaces. Clad in dark smoked oak and attended by a family of pendant lights, the bar counter is a stimulating and dramatic visual element. A second glance renders visible the special lighting effects and intricate patterning of the wall coverings with their delicate floral motifs, including designs tailored especially for the bar.

A rapturous combination – nature meets glamour in playful materiality.

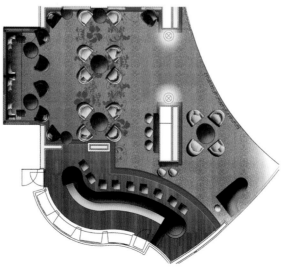

Hilton Munich Park
Germany

Restaurant
Hotel Category: ★ ★ ★ ★
Hotel Type: Business hotel
Size: 484 rooms
The Brief: Complete renovation: development of a design concept for the restaurant 'Tivoli'
Total floor space: Restaurant 390 m², buffet 133 m²
Seats: 184; additional seats in the pavilion
Finalist: European Hospitality Award 2012

Local color is at its best when applied in subtle interpretations that will delight guests upon their discovery. The discrete use of regional design elements is the secret behind the enchantingly warm spirit that welcomes guests within this space. This atmosphere defines the Tivoli restaurant, with an experience that literally begins the moment guests step foot inside, where an oak table with turned accents marks the reception and staging area. Behind the table, wardrobe doors upholstered in soft leather with fine white seams adorning their surfaces – a tribute to that most Bavarian of apparel, the Lederhose. Inside, guests move through the buffet zone – shielded from view in the evening by fine drapery –

proceeding gallantly to their tables. Warm shades of brown, beige and orange fill the room, combined with elements of dark smoked oak and its lighter counterpart, with organic forms setting a tone of understatement in a pleasantly stylish ambience. To the side, decorative laser cuts illuminate the wood paneling, setting off the interior. In another nod to Bavarian culture, the pendant lights suspended above the Captain's Table are inspired by the style of cartwheel once popular in this region.

Sumptuous leather, delicate seams and the finest craftsmanship – details make all the difference.

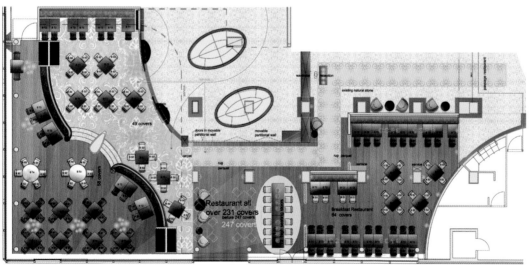

Restaurant all
over 231 covers
before 247 covers
247 covers

Breakfast Restaurant
64 covers

58 covers

49 covers

Home of Sports Hamburg
Germany

Lobby
Hotel Category: ★ ★ ★
Hotel Type: Sports hotel
Size: 153 rooms
The Brief: New building: development of a design concept for the lobby
Total floor space: 221.30 m²
Seats: 55

A new sports center is in development on the outskirts of Hamburg close to the city's largest stadiums – with direct access to a fitness club, this sports hotel is set to drive the center's appeal through the roof. The target audience: sports enthusiasts, fitness fanatics and all those with athletic aspirations. The young and the young-at-heart will feel at home here: the hotel is a place to talk shop with like-minded individuals, to compare training plans and finishing times, to swap tales of challenges new and old – and after a grueling training session, guests can unwind and indulge their culinary whims with a few drinks in good company, play darts or clean up on the foosball table.

With its cozy armchairs and fireplace, the lobby serves as a tranquil refuge. Fresh and natural colors inform the atmosphere, complemented by plenty of glass and lighting of various qualities. And for those who simply can't get enough time on the field with their friends: acoustic glass panels separate the games lounge, where tireless athletes can face-off over foosball or billiards. The photo-frames on the glass partitioning wall invite guests to stand proud alongside the heroes of German sporting history in a very personal Hall of Fame – the crowd goes wild!

Back to the future – faces of the past and present.

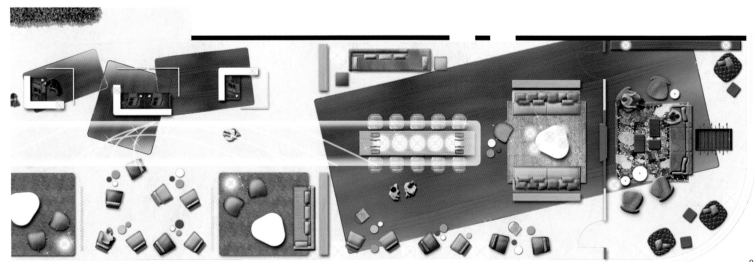

Home of Sports Hamburg
Germany

Bar

Hotel Category: ★ ★ ★ ★
Hotel Type: Sports hotel
Size: 153 rooms
The Brief: New building: development of a design concept for the bar
Total floor space: 152.90 m²
Seats: 47

The bar at this sports hotel has plenty more to offer than vitamin cocktails… A wide range of health drinks are available, but guests looking to wrap up their day with a soothing herbal bitter will not be disappointed. The bar is the ideal place to celebrate victories with fellow team members, discuss strategies for on and off the field, and indulge in stirring memories of goals scored and games lost. What's the right look for a bar for light refreshments?

The bar is at the epicenter of this space – a linchpin and hub of activity. Entering the room, guests discover a green oasis, complemented by the lush vegetation of a living wall. To the side, lighting fixtures adorn the wall like blossoms – nature is a tangible presence here, coupled with hi-tech materials and a cutting-edge lighting system. A series of red ribbons circumnavigate the bar counter, while red lampshades hover above in a moment of playful aesthetic symmetry. In a fitting tribute to athletic history, the bar stools take their cue from the traditional vaulting box.

A bar with a refreshing view onto the past.

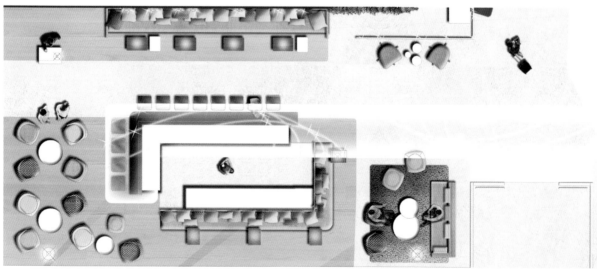

Home of Sports Hamburg
Germany

Restaurant
Hotel Category: ★ ★ ★ ★
Hotel Type: Sports hotel
Size: 153 rooms
The Brief: New building: development of a design concept for the restaurant
Total floor space: Restaurant 220 m², buffet 18 m²
Seats: 124

Fit for fun: a place to indulge in good food. A restaurant for athletes and sports enthusiasts to freshen up and regain their strength. It is a gas station for the body and the soul. The restaurant welcomes guests every morning with a generous buffet of fresh foods. Individual tables are available for guests traveling alone, alongside long common tables for informal get-togethers. For those who prefer to begin the day in silence, newspapers and sports magazines are close to hand in the integrated holders.

The atmosphere is informal and uncomplicated – mornings and evenings. The foundation: a natural canon. A sprinkling of color teases the senses. On the home straight – the ribbon lining the walls holds the room together. Tailored seating elements serve a range of purposes, with chairs, benches, ottomans and wing chairs on hand for mid-morning coffee. This patchwork landscape is rich in fine accents and reminiscences on sporting history. Here, too, the tongue-in-cheek design of the vaulting box stools gives guests cause to chuckle.

Where tradition and *Zeitgeist* meet.

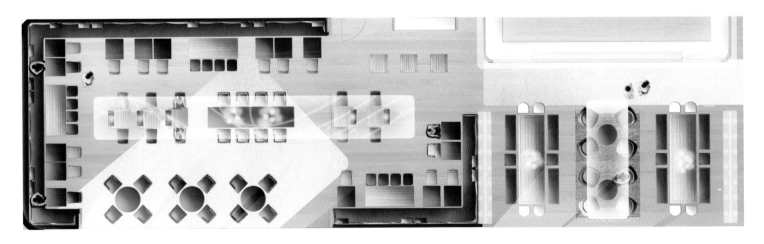

Hotel Ritter Durbach
Germany

Lobby
Hotel Category: ★ ★ ★ ★ superior
Hotel Type: Spa hotel
Size: 60 rooms
The Brief: Renovation: development of a design concept for the lobby
Total floor space: 138 m²
Seats: 32

Somewhat smaller private hotels are the pearls of the hotel industry. Here you find individuality, personality and esprit dominated by the special people who run them and a history that often goes back a few hundred years. In Durbach, Germany, nestled in the middle of vineyards at the edge of the Black Forest, is one of these pearls – the Hotel Ritter.

Dealing in a sensitive way with the traditional charm of this hotel was important for the design concept. It needed combine the modern and the traditional in a harmonious way. Typical objects from the surrounding region were newly interpreted to realize this, old props newly polished as it were. One of these is a real highlight in the reception area – a fuchsia colored wall with a modern interpretation of the white cuckoo clock, naturally made in the Black Forest. There is a bit of playfulness in the design as well. The lobby, dominated by brown and crème tones, has a pink sofa in a floral pattern from grandma's time in it. There are pictures on the wall behind the sofa, a wall of fame with pictures of famous guests from earlier times like former German president Richard von Weizsäcker, François Mitterand, Helmut Kohl, the Dalai Lama and a host of famous actors.

A modern knight – a skillful unity of the traditional and the modern.

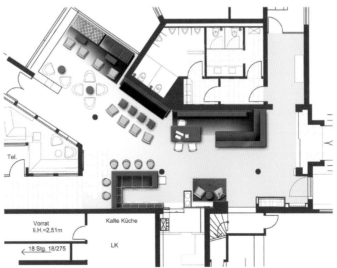

Hotel Ritter Durbach
Germany

Gourmet Restaurant
Hotel Category: ★ ★ ★ ★ superior
Hotel Type: Spa hotel
Size: 60 rooms
The Brief: Renovation: development of a design concept for the restaurant 'Wilder Ritter'
Total floor space: 315.70 m²
Seats: 100
One Michelin Star

The beautiful surrounds were inspiration for making wine a recurring theme of the design concept for the Wilder Ritter restaurant, which boasts a 350 year history. Colors and materials used in the restaurant evoke Riesling and Pinot Noir wines – an appropriate setting for the restaurant's outstanding kitchen, which was awarded a Michelin star in just its first year.

The Wilder Ritter gourmet restaurant has wallpaper that was specially made for this project and decorated by hand with silver leaf in fine-wine motifs that demonstrates how important the red and white wines are for the hotel. Here again are details that playfully evoke the long tradition of the hotel – like the picture of a bellowing stag in one of the dining areas, or the row of small antlers in another. Use of warm apple wood veneer with special inlay images adds cozy warmth to the partially offset spaces that make up the restaurant.

Fresh Riesling and a full-bodied Pinot Noir translated into color, form and ambience.

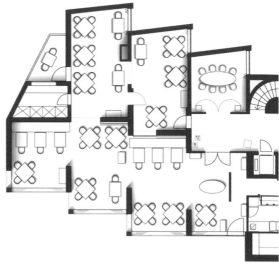

JW Marriott Cannes
France

Entrance

Hotel Category: ★ ★ ★ ★ ★ luxury

Hotel Type: City resort hotel

Size: 261 rooms

The Brief: Renovation: development of a design concept for the entrance area (outside)

Total floor space: 264.60 m²

Cannes is a location blessed by the sun. Here you can enjoy life to the fullest, strolling down the famous La Croisette, sitting in a café or bar with a summer cocktail or glass of champagne, while looking out upon the sunlit sea, the golden beach and palm trees.

The JW Marriot Cannes in the Palais Stéphanie is one of the most exclusive of its kind between the Mediterranean and the southern Alps. The renovation of the outer entrance reflects the brand, as do all the other renovated public spaces in the hotel. The outer entrance should symbolize the uniqueness of the hotel and luxury that guests expect and find actually here. The golden roof design is a reference to the palm of the famous film festival and leads guests with its various fan-like motifs into the hotel with glittering aplomb. Guests might not walk into the hotel on a red carpet but over something just as wonderful – black marble. A golden band carries forth the color of the palm-shaped roof and shows guest the way to the interior of the hotel.

A hotel that seduces its guests with cinematic motifs.

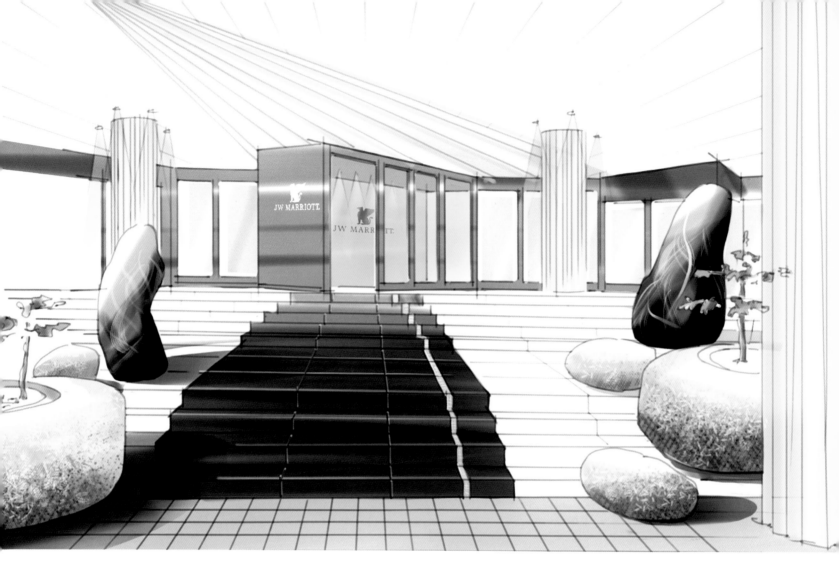

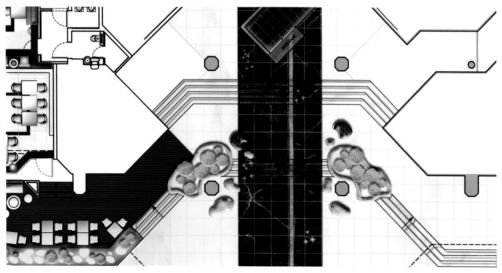

JW Marriott Cannes
France

Lobby & Bar
Hotel Category: ★ ★ ★ ★ ★ luxury
Hotel Type: City resort hotel
Size: 261 rooms
The Brief: Renovation: development of a design concept for the lobby and bar
Total floor space: 407.30 m²
Seats: 78

The design on the outside entrance of the hotel is continued on the inside. Here is an interior dominated by uncomplicated elegance, with a subdued and inviting ambience and the highest levels of luxurious comfort.

The hotel's entrance hall is several stories high and so impressively monumental and imposing that it almost looks like church architecture. Yet you are never overwhelmed by its size. This is realized by an elaborate lighting installation consisting of more than 1,600 golden plates, delicate and leaf-like, which stretches out overhead at a height of 22 meters and transforms the concert hall-like space into cozier dimensions. High-quality white marble on the walls and on

the floor is combined with black, gold and brown elements to create a lightness and warmth, while pushing the edged massiveness of the reception area into the background. An open bar with a host of seating options to choose from. You can relax in a modern winged easy chair, or drink a cocktail at the bar in a high, gold painted bar stool with in organic design language. This bar is a meeting place day and night, right in the middle of Cannes where you can enjoy the city's famous nightlight or watch celebrities have fun. And not only during the famous film festival.

A hotel offering pure luxury combined with honest understatement.

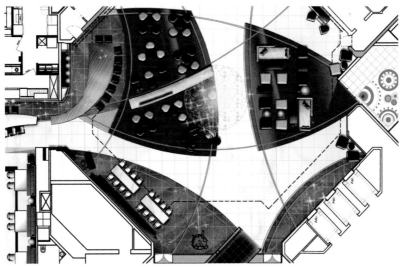

JW Marriott Cannes
France

Restaurant
Hotel Category: ★ ★ ★ ★ ★ luxury
Hotel Type: City resort hotel
Size: 261 rooms
The Brief: Renovation: development of a design concept for the specialty restaurant 'JW Grill'
Total floor space: 205.50 m²
Seats: 77

When a restaurant already has everything for hours of unforgettable fine dining, it only needs the right backdrop to be perfect. And this is exactly what the high art of a tailor-made design concept can do.

In renovating this restaurant the challenge was to visually point the way for guests in the lobby to the restaurant and make it easier to see. The solution was in the design and placement of the so-called communal table – a central element of the brand concept. This was specially made with white slabs of marble, placed in a seemingly random manner in relation to each other, to form the shape of a modern table. Its placement at the end of the bar counter makes it visible from the lobby and looking at it automatically leads your eyes directly to the restaurant. Here you will find pure indulgence for palate and eyes. The overall design concept is carried forth here with a fascinating light sculpture, highest-quality materials like rust-brown leather with finely quilted seams, dark golden upholstered fabrics, white leather seats with handmade rivet edging and once again white marble for the floors – here interspersed with black.

Vive la France – a treat for your palate and your eyes.

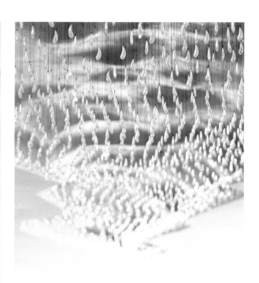

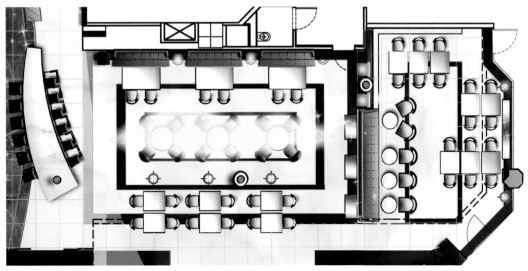

Kavalier Palais Vienna
Austria

Lobby
Hotel Category: ★ ★ ★ ★ ★ luxury
Hotel Type: City hotel
Size: 221 rooms
The Brief: Renovation: development of a design concept for the lobby
Total floor space: 313.10 m²
Seats: 21

Vienna – the city of Empress Sisi, the Vienna Opera and Philharmonic Orchestra, the waltzes of Johann Strauss, the world famous Sachertorte – is also a city of horse-drawn carriages that keep the past alive as they carry visitors through the streets to various landmarks. Today's popular Spanish Riding School is living witness to the fact that horses have always been of special importance to city on the Danube.

You get a sense of this tradition upon entering the newly-designed lobby of this grand hotel. Not at first glance perhaps, but if you look closer you'll clearly see –

rising from the first floor to the upper floor – a myriad of shimmering crystals tracing the silhouette of a jumping horse whose upward movement points to additional public areas on the second floor. Proud, powerful and elegant, this sculpture is a contemporary interpretation of local history celebrating the hotel and its roots in this magical city.

The greatest joy on earth is found on the back of a horse – homage to the famous steeds of Vienna.

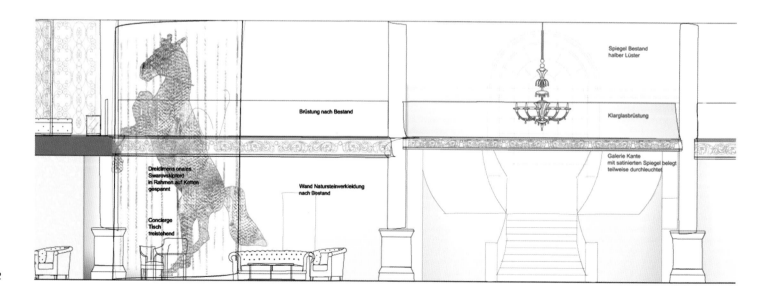

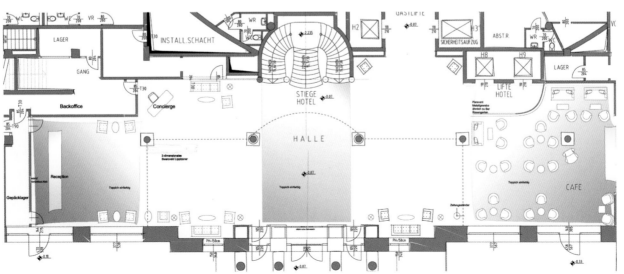

103

Kavalier Palais Vienna
Austria

Bar
Hotel Category: ★ ★ ★ ★ ★ luxury
Hotel Type: City hotel
Size: 221 rooms
The Brief: Renovation: development of a design concept for the 'Kavalier Bar'
Total floor space: 80.40 m²
Seats: 34

There is no better place for fine dining after a full program of sightseeing, or for a nightcap after an enchanting evening at the opera, than the gallery of this grand hotel. It possesses a uniquely Viennese ambiance where tradition is still a part of everyday life. The past is everywhere and you can almost hear the clattering hooves from carriages rolling down narrow streets when you enter the bar.

The bottles and glasses cupboard with backlighting at the back of the bar is in the shape of one of these horses, traced in a fine line. The atmosphere is subdued and immerses the space in soft nuances of green mixing with reflecting mirrored surfaces and the glow of chandeliers. A nod to the modern is given by transparent cubic forms for tables and counters with backlighting, which create an exciting contrast to the bar's comfortable wingback, deep-buttoned easy chairs. At the back there are niches with high-back seats that guarantee an intimate conversation for two, whereby the wall design here is also dominated by horse motifs.

Cognac between buggies and horse-drawn carriages – a bar perfect for Vienna.

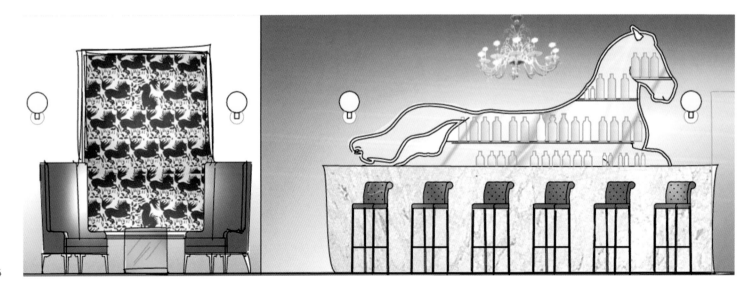

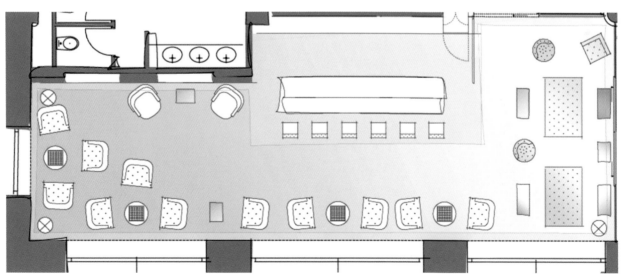

Kokenhof Großburgwedel
Germany

Reception with Lobby Bar
Hotel Category: ★ ★ ★ ★
Hotel Type: Conference and countryside hotel
Size: 44 rooms
The Brief: Renovation: development of a design concept for the reception with lobby bar
Total floor space: Lobby 73.70 m², bar 77.90 m²
Seats: Lobby 13, bar 42

This hotel is a timber-framed structure from 1556. The wooden beams of the original structure were at one time to be shipped to the USA and rebuilt there but the plan fell through and the large country estate was built in Großburgwedel instead. It is now used for conference guests, wedding parties, wellness aficionados and fans of gourmet dining. In the past the inside was like a farmhouse parlor at the front – a lot of dark wood, heavy furniture, an old fireplace and a lot of white walls. The complete renovation of the hotel's public spaces contains references to this but with modern elements, and always with respect to the original interior.
The results of the renovation reveal a mix of yesterday and today, a design that integrates contemporary forms and materials in the historical structure. Backlit glass cubes where guests are individually checked in at reception represent one of these contemporary elements. A rust-colored rear wall here symbolizes the 'today' aspect of the design but the material is in old-world patina look. And the prettiest bridge from the past to the present is the natural Solnhofen stone slabs on the floor which were part of the original interior. They were carefully removed, cleaned and – after a floor-heating system was installed – placed back into their original spots.

Sign of the times – a hotel between yesterday and today.

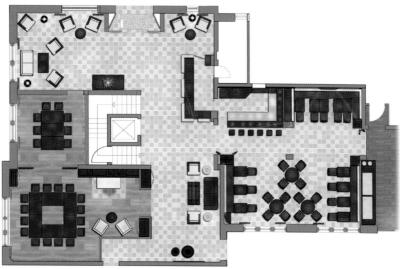

Le Clervaux
Luxembourg

Restaurant
Hotel Category: ★ ★ ★ ★
Hotel Type: Boutique hotel
Size: 22 suites
The Brief: Renovation: development of a design concept for the restaurant 'Da Lonati'
Total floor space: 75 m²
Seats: 34
Boutique Media: Boutique Design Award 2012, category 'Most surprising visual element'
Heinze Verlag: First Place Popular Vote 2013
Iconic Awards 2013: category 'Interior – Hospitality'

Deep in the Clerve Valley and in the middle of the Arde region of northern Luxembourg is the picturesque village of Clervaux, which never fails to enchant visitors with its Medieval charm. Embedded in these unique surroundings is this boutique hotel. All areas of the hotel were renovated in the design of a modern grand hotel. To achieve this, a play of Baroque elements were newly interpreted and used.

Upon entering the Da Lonati restaurant, the first thing you see is a new glass façade which has flooded the room in daylight since renovation. The restaurant itself is divided into two areas – an all-day dining area and a fine-dining area. Eye-catcher in the all-day

dining area is a red wall with large mirrors in playfully designed white frames behind a long upholstered bench. Creating a fascinating contrast to this are the white flanking walls with half-height waffle paneling. On one of these side walls, positioned above the painted wall paneling, is a large Baroque pattern made of colored wine corks. Above the tables in front of the upholstered bench are decorative Plexiglas lamps in red that shine with a cozy warmth, while ceiling projections overhead lend the entire restaurant a discreet and relaxed ambience.

Dining at the Da Lonati – a modern interpretation of Baroque pomp.

 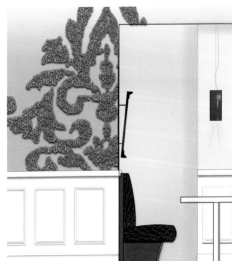 

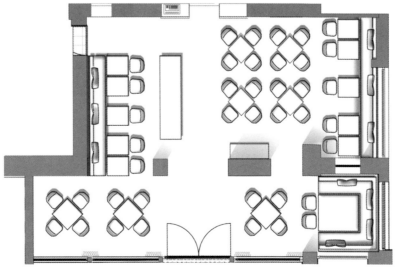

Le Clervaux
Luxembourg

Restaurant / Fine Dining
Hotel Category: ★ ★ ★ ★ ★
Hotel Type: Boutique hotel
Size: 22 suites
The Brief: Renovation: development of a design concept for the fine dining restaurant
Total floor space: 70.90 m²
Seats: 36

Boutique Media: Boutique Design Award 2012, category 'Most surprising visual element'
Heinze Verlag: First Place Popular Vote 2013
Iconic Awards 2013: category 'Interior – Hospitality'

The design concept goal was to integrate the original manorial ambience into the new design by employing subtle details and to use individual elements of the original interior again. Here you are welcomed by a sophisticated atmosphere that, due to its stylish interpretation, is not flamboyant or excessive but rather hints at its extravagant character.

Although the fine dining area of the restaurant has an overall design that's somewhat subtler in its use of color, with more classic elements, than the all-day dining area, it is perfectly integrated into the concept nonetheless. The grey wall paneling of wood with white structural molding gives the space a timeless feel. The individual and mobile walls for partitioning the restaurant are designed in the same way, whereby the spatial unity seems to disappear. The design of the carpet pays homage to the hotel's past with a historical tile pattern from the entrance area of the restaurant. The furniture with its large Baroque patterns in high-quality materials made with fine craftsmanship makes an elegant impression. Indirect cove lighting overhead adds a friendly touch.

A contemporary interpretation of the sophisticated ambience.

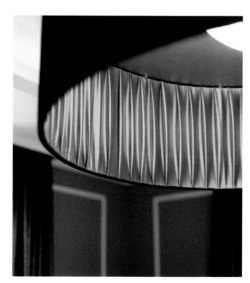

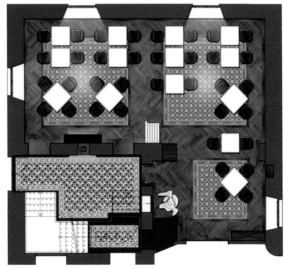

Le Clervaux
Luxembourg

Breakfast Restaurant

Hotel Category: ★ ★ ★ ★ ★

Hotel Type: Boutique hotel

Size: 22 suites

The Brief: Renovation: development of a design concept for the breakfast restaurant

Total floor space: Restaurant 143.70 m², buffet 37 m²

Seats: 96

Boutique Media: Boutique Design Award 2012, category 'Most surprising visual element'
Heinze Verlag: First Place Popular Vote 2013
Iconic Awards 2013:
category 'Interior – Hospitality'

The design of this boutique hotel's public areas and its suites is sometimes more in the direction of Baroque sophistication, and sometimes in a more modern direction with fashionable elements, contemporary colors and shapes. But always with the goal that you find yourself in a modern hotel with a design that reflects the spirit of the age. While eating an ample breakfast to get refreshed and ready for a new day, the breakfast restaurant offers you surroundings with some Baroque elements that nonetheless glow with a certain youthfulness through the design's use of color and shapes. Warm gray and beige tones combined with red accents – like the carpet design – make for an elegant, cozy ambience full of energy. One of the highlights here is a red band made up of carpet and wallpaper created especially for this purpose that – both with the same floral pattern –surrounds the wall of windows like a giant ribbon around a glass façade. Daylight shining into this glass façade provides additional refreshment and inspires you to explore the area around the hotel after breakfast.

The right start to a new day – the younger face of the Baroque.

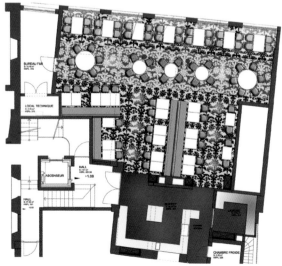

Le Méridien Grand Hotel Nuremberg, Germany

Restaurant

Hotel Category: ★ ★ ★ ★

Hotel Type: City hotel (built at the turn of the last century)

Size: 192 rooms

The Brief: Renovation: development of a design concept for the restaurant 'Fürstenhof'

Total floor space: 137.60 m²

Seats: 69

A hotel from the turn of the nineteenth century – the Grand Hotel is situated directly vis à vis the central railway terminus. Glamorous balls were once held in its halls. This spirit of grandeur is still tangible. With a sensitive makeover of the rooms now complete, the time had come to bring change to the public spaces: the revitalization of the Fürstenhof restaurant for private functions and special occasions breathed fresh life into the interior, rejuvenating the space while paying tribute to its origins.

The houndstooth pattern made world-famous by Coco Chanel's jackets – a gesture to the French roots of the Le Méridien brand that now also graces the guest rooms – is reflected here in the black and white accents of the coffered wall panels and frames the presentation of the restaurant's appealing new wall coverings. Fine lines traverse the restaurant's flooring, illuminated from above by an undulating sea of chrome orbs, creating a setting with the flexibility to host a variety of seating arrangements.

A restaurant pays homage to Coco Chanel.

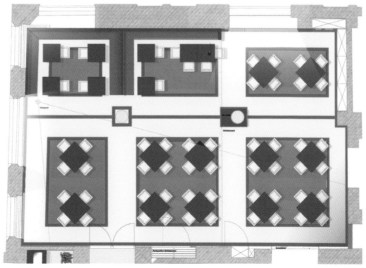

Le Méridien Parkhotel Frankfurt M., Germany

Lobby
Hotel Category: ★ ★ ★ ★
Hotel Type: City hotel
Size: 297 rooms
The Brief: Complete refurbishment: development of a design concept for the lobby
Total floor space: 145.50 m²
Seats: 13
Adex Platinum Award 2009

Just a short walk from the central railway terminus: Le Méridien Parkhotel on Wiesenhüttenplatz – the lobby of Frankfurt's Grande Dame has always been popular with the city's high society as a venue to celebrate family occasions and paint the town red. A comprehensive makeover of the building provided an opportunity to revitalize the interior with contemporary accents while taking care to preserve the hotel's historical character. A meeting place for the modern world: this new presentation embodies a modern attitude with a respectful perspective that honors the building's past. The interior design is a combination of the old and the new. The hotel's commitment to modern customer service is underscored by the separate reception islands. The message is clear: our guests are individuals, not just numbers. Classical furniture elements such as the Coconut Chair add to the stylish ambience, demonstrating a heightened sensibility towards tradition and an affinity for artistic design. Tranquil moments in the urban jungle: leather upholstered wall panels and subdued lighting exude an aura of timeless elegance and soothing beauty.

The lobby – a stylish refuge in the big city.

Le Méridien Parkhotel Frankfurt M., Germany

Bar

Hotel Category: ★ ★ ★ ★
Hotel Type: City hotel
Size: 297 rooms
The Brief: Complete refurbishment: development of a design concept for the 'Casablanca Bar'
Total floor space: 106.60 m²
Seats: 42

Humphrey Bogart would feel at home in this bar which pays tribute to one of the greatest scenes in film history. There's a harsh wind blowing in the city of stock brokers and high finance. Buy or sell – sometimes every second counts. During the day, the restless urgency of the financial markets sets the tone in the inner city, and come evening it's a pleasure to sip on a refreshing drink at the bar. Leaving business at the door, guests come here to unwind, mingle with the crowd and shrug off the cares of the workday. The interior offers a welcome escape as it spirits guests away into the colorful and exotic world of Morocco's largest city on the Atlantic Coast. Creating a broad range of individual lighting moods was a particular focus of this renovation, resulting in a warm and radiant ambience. From the iridescent golden mosaic tiles to the beaded metal curtains and the bar's vibrant cushions and ottomans – this is Casablanca. The bar's myriad lamps and lighting fixtures cast a menagerie of shadows against the walls while studded leather armchairs transport us into a distant time and place.

'Here's looking at you, kid.' A bar with an evocative look.

118

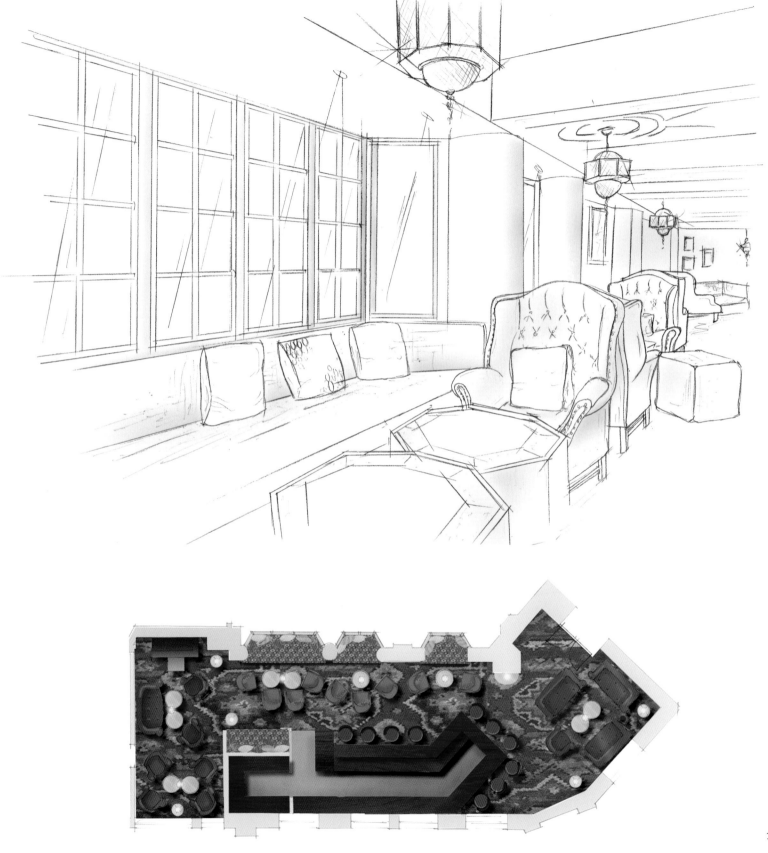

Les Jardins d'Alysea, Roeser
Luxembourg

Lobby
Category: ★ ★ ★ ★ ★
Type: Senior residence
Size: 250 rooms
The Brief: New building: development of a design concept for the lobby
Total floor space: 106.50 m²
Seats: 11

Children's songs still recall how a famous variety of rose was grown here and exported throughout the world. A wonderful tradition that was forgotten far too soon. For this newly-built luxury residence the objective was to create a warm and unique reception area with a calm spatial feel that prepares guests for a luxurious and private stay.

The interior takes up the motif of growing roses and fondly plays with the theme. Some design details can be discovered only after a second look – a relief in fabric or the wood-carved surface of furniture can be touched, for instance. Discovering these things yourself makes these details even more memorable; you tell people about them and recommend the hotel to friends and acquaintances. The design objective here is to create a surprisingly modern interpretation of a classic ambience that represents the sophistication and tradition of the hotel. An eye-catcher is the corridor's wood paneling whose surface seems to dissolve away to reveal tendrils of roses growing across the wall.

Classic meets modernity – in surprising combinations.

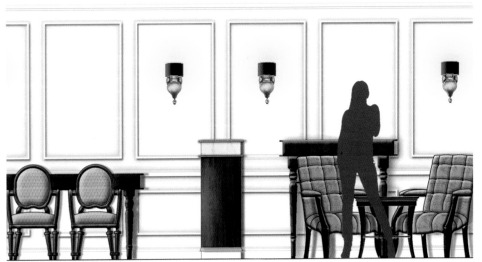

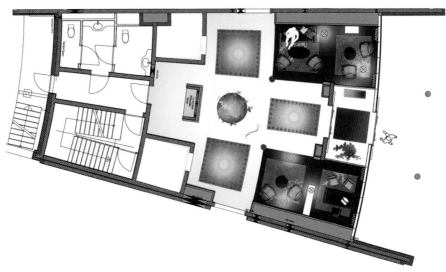

Les Jardins d'Alysea, Roeser
Luxembourg

Restaurant / Private Dining
Category: ★ ★ ★ ★ ★
Type: Senior residence
Size: 250 rooms
The Brief: New building: development of a design concept for the private dining restaurant
Total floor space: 85 m²
Seats: 26

Dining in a private, refined atmosphere with a view onto the garden and the natural surroundings. This is one of several different private dining areas that guests can choose, for two or for smaller groups. Important for the private spaces here – there should not be too many tables and they should be set far enough apart so guests can dine and talk undisturbed.

The interior concept takes up differentiating the dining areas with the floor design. The personal atmosphere that extends throughout the residence can also be felt here. Pictures with different frames and hung in salon style underscore this feel-

ing of privacy. Wainscots along the walls with built-in cupboards and glass cabinets evoke a sense of being at home. Guests can discover a lot here if they take a closer look – floral motifs in homage to the rose growing that dominated this location in the past can be found on the insides of the lampshades, for instance, and in the intarsia found between the parquet and carpeting.

A restaurant with personality.

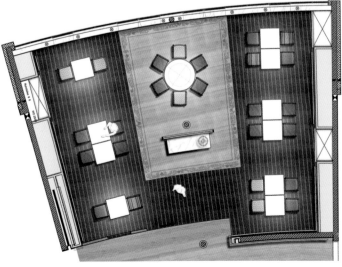

Lindner Park-Hotel Hagenbeck
Hamburg, Germany

Lobby

Hotel Category: ★ ★ ★ ★

Hotel Type: Urban hotel

Size: 134 rooms

The Brief: New building: development of a design concept for the lobby

Total floor space: 112.40 m²

Seats: 12

hotelforum: Hotelimmobilie des Jahres 2009 (hotel property of the year)

In the distance, the muted call of a giraffe. Closer by, an elephant trumpets in the night. Located well within earshot of a safari park close by the city of Hamburg, guests at this remarkable hotel enjoy close up views of exotic wildlife. The hotel is ideal not just for animal lovers and families with children, but also for business travelers keen to recharge their batteries and seek inspiration for their future endeavors – or to escape for a time from the earnest world of pocket squares, pinstripes, and price points. While the interiors of the guest rooms take their cues from the native countries of the park's exotic wildlife, the public area on the ground floor is presented in Colonial Style, complete with a vast collection of souvenirs from around the world. Casual furniture invites guests to linger. Stylish maritime elevators with external LED displays connect the public area with the guest rooms above. Travel from one continent to the next – with an interior design inspired by a ship's cabin from the age of sail, the elevators act as a unifying element, linking the two worlds in a playful reference to the journeys undertaken by the magnificent creatures nearby.

Take a trip around the world with this hotel.

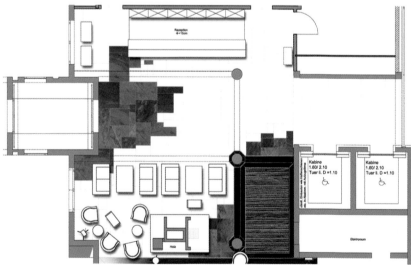

Lindner Park-Hotel Hagenbeck
Hamburg, Germany

Bar
Hotel Category: ★ ★ ★ ★
Hotel Type: Urban hotel
Size: 134 rooms
The Brief: New building: development of a design concept for the bar
Total floor space: 109.20 m²
Seats: 43
hotelforum: Hotelimmobilie des Jahres 2009 (hotel property of the year)

'Take five' and enjoy a refreshing drink. Oozing with colonial charm and situated directly adjacent to the hotel lobby, the sumptuous bar. Hosted on the grounds of the famous safari park, extraordinary experiences await guests inside this hotel dedicated to the wonders of the animal kingdom. From Africa to Asia and the Arctic, the safari park is home to wildlife from around the world – guests will learn everything there is to known about their origins and natural habits. The bar's unique atmosphere makes it the ideal place to prepare for a visit to the zoo or to take time out from a busy schedule to freshen up between meetings.

At the bar, bottles are presented against a back-lit screen of carved wood behind a counter fronted with ornate relief work. Upholstered in heavy red leather, bar stools flank this element in a response to the lobby's luxurious armchairs. Soothing music, coffered paneling, diffuse lighting and rustic parquetry flooring complete the picture, while ornamental elements bring the animal kingdom into the interior. This is the way to unwind – with a journey to faraway places.

Welcome to the animal kingdom – a bar with character.

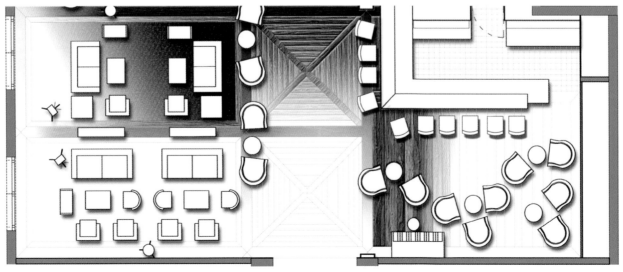

Lindner Park-Hotel Hagenbeck
Hamburg, Germany

Restaurant

Hotel Category: ★ ★ ★ ★
Hotel Type: Urban hotel
Size: 134 rooms
The Brief: New building: development of a design concept for the restaurant
Total floor space: Restaurant 377.20 m², buffet 103 m²
Seats: 217
hotelforum: Hotelimmobilie des Jahres 2009 (hotel property of the year)

Arriving at the reception, guests of this hotel are queried about their preferences. An Asian room, perhaps? Or something African? The wellness area transports guests to the Arctic realms of the polar bear. Public areas are best served by more neutral terrain that will not overshadow the experiences on offer elsewhere in the hotel. The Colonial Style implemented here is a perfect fit – its capacious, cosmopolitan and welcoming presentation brings together an untold number of souvenirs from journeys to the seven continents.

The restaurant delights with relief carvings of African elephants, figurines and busts from Asia and columns adorned with capitals from faraway places. Large classical ceiling fans and a combination of tiger oak and natural stone floor surfaces frames the picture. Carved sliding panels shield the large buffet zone of an evening and early-risers can pick up their breakfast-to-go here before departing to the airport. A long high table serves as a staging area for guests and provides a decorative surface in the evening.

Dine in the company of elephants and giraffes – a restaurant in a safari park.

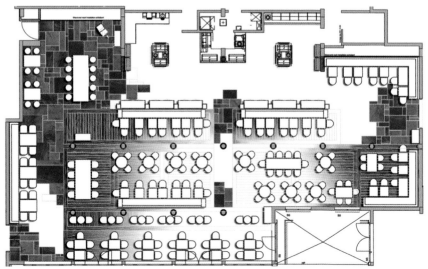

Marina Place Split
Croatia

Lobby

Hotel Category: ★ ★ ★ ★

Hotel Type: Resort and conference hotel

Size: 314 rooms

The Brief: Revitalization: development of a design concept for the lobby

Total floor space: 490.70 m²

Seats: 20

Located directly at the yacht marina in Split, this brilliant white tower hotel was built in General Tito's Yugoslavia and known back then as playground for the rich and famous. After revitalization with a new organization, it now includes a large adjacent conference and event center. Not only does it possess the allure of a beach holiday, it also lets you spend your days in unique surroundings – the Mediterranean in deep blue, every kind of seafood, luxury yachts and a fresh sea breeze combine here for a truly unforgettable stay.

The hotel's spacious lobby with large glass front looking out on the marina inspires guests to walk around and get their bearings, to feel at home, meet friends, schedule meetings. This modern structure demands a contemporary elegance. Here you should be attuned to the where you are – water and waves everywhere. An ocean of shimmering pilasters in the floor, glass and natural stone fronts like the marina docks stroked by waves, and the eye-catcher looking up – a waterfall of Swarovski crystals in the center of a curved staircase in black glass.

The color of the water – elegance to the sound of sea waves.

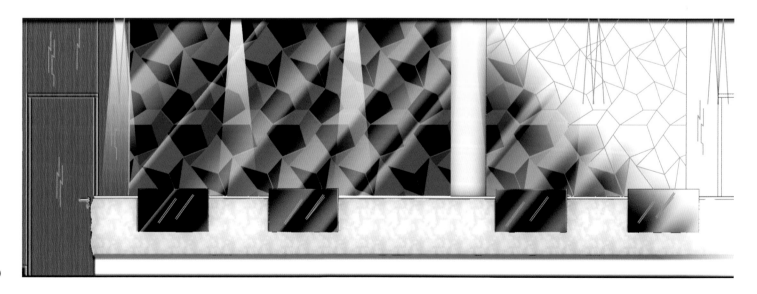

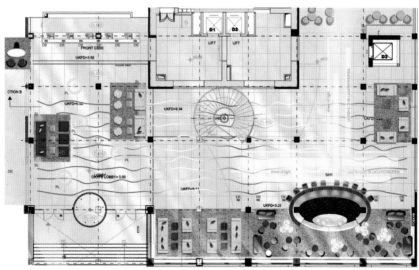

Marina Place Split
Croatia

Lobby Bar

Hotel Category: ★ ★ ★ ★ ★

Hotel Type: Resort and conference hotel

Size: 314 rooms

The Brief: Revitalization: development of a design concept for the lobby bar

Total floor space: 128 m²

Seats: 48

Located in the spacious entrance hall is your first refuge, your first oasis – the lobby bar. Here you receive your welcome drink and make plans for your stay. You have a clear view of the marina. What's happening out there? Who's meeting whom? Where can I go clubbing? It isn't an easy task to redesign a freestanding bar, in the field of view of the façade, to be an appealing place to meet people and have fun. How do you attract guests without blocking the view too much?

The answer? Transparency. All the seats at the bar are aligned to give a great view outside. And this view is unobstructed by the back wall made of glass in the middle of the bar structure. You can see between the bottles and follow what's happening outside. The lobby bar is incorporated into its surroundings like a seashell integrated in ocean waves. Bubbles of air seem to rise. Bottles and glasses are placed in round shelves that create a wave-like movement that is picked up and enhanced by the ceiling lighting. A bar for light enjoyment – just seeing it makes you want a sparkling drink.

A bar like a seashell – ocean view included.

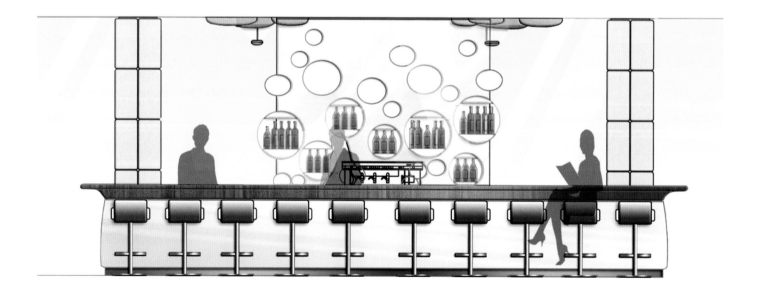

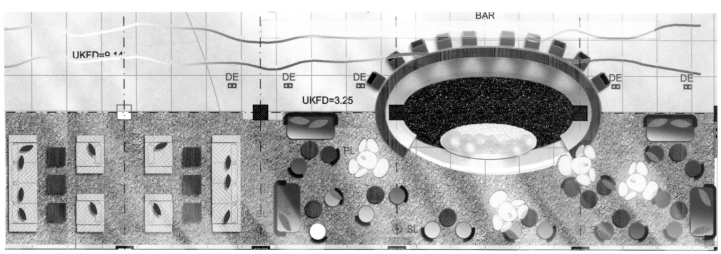

Marina Place Split
Croatia

Bar
Hotel Category: ★ ★ ★ ★
Hotel Type: Resort and conference hotel
Size: 314 rooms
The Brief: Revitalization: development of a design concept for the bar
Total floor space: 198.70 m²
Seats: 38

Upstairs is the lobby bar's big brother. Up here, set somewhat apart from the hustle-bustle in the lobby, it also offers a view of the marina with additional tables on the terrace under open skies. This level also has access to the conference rooms. The special task here is to make the bar noticeable even when there isn't an event being held. A restaurant on an upper floor is always a challenge. With ever new floor, the chance that guests make the effort to come here drops.

The concept creates two effects using a single design element. A sea of wind-filled sails, that is also reminiscent of a flock of birds, provides protection and reflects the proportions of the lobby spaces below. You can literally hear the seagull's cry. At the same time, their open wings create a visual link upwards, inspiring curiosity and giving an airy touch to a bar designed with maritime flair. Its wooden cladding reminiscent of boat building, a bar shaped like a boat's hull and seats like beach chairs literally invite guests in.

A bar with sails and seagulls.

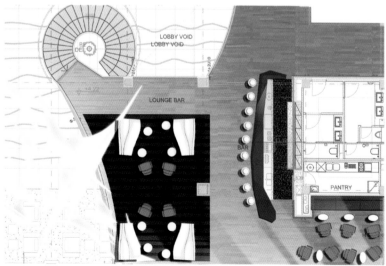

Marina Place Split
Croatia

Restaurant
Hotel Category: ★ ★ ★ ★ ★
Hotel Type: Resort and conference hotel
Size: 314 rooms
The Brief: Revitalization: development of a design concept for the buffet restaurant
Total floor space: Restaurant 498.50 m², buffet 115.80 m²
Seats: 267; plus overflow area: 186

Ah, the agony of choice! For guests vacationing at this luxury hotel there are several dining options. The large buffet restaurant serves a rich and extensive breakfast every morning with nothing left to the imagination. When the hotel is fully booked up, there's even a so-called 'overflow area' in addition to this which otherwise remains closed. The goal here is to remove the massiveness of the room and to create an atmosphere that does justice to a hotel of this category.

The interior design concept makes this possible. Guests enter as if boarding a cruise ship, a luxury liner, and make themselves comfortable. There are seats with nautical railings, and some with a view onto a coral reef. Windows look like those at the front of a ship's cabin. There are mariner's lamps, high-gloss paint and ship's parquet. You drift in the world of seafaring and lean back to relax. Add to this the lagoon in sight, full speed ahead. Flowing forms wash over you and you don't want to leave again.

A restaurant like a cruise on the ocean.

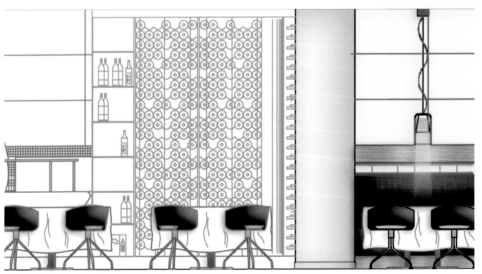

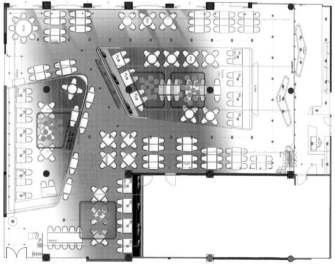

Marina Place Split
Croatia

**Gourmet Restaurant
and Champagne Bar**
Hotel Category: ★ ★ ★ ★
Hotel Type: Resort and conference hotel
Size: 314 rooms
The Brief: Revitalization: development of
a design concept for the gourmet restaurant and champagne bar
Total floor space: Restaurant 260.40 m²,
bar 122.20 m²
Seats: Restaurant 108, bar 42

Seafood and champagne are an ideal combination – yet this location adds a sense of authenticity that makes it truly special. Look out of the panorama windows onto the marina, watch the fishing boats come back to harbor in the evening next to the elegant yacht marina to unload their day's catch. And all these ocean delicacies will then make it onto the menu – you can't have it any more authentic and fresh than this. This freshness is discreetly enhanced by the interior design. Guests are immersed in an underwater world with an aquarium flanking the entranceway and a continuous wave created by strands made of glittering crystals that give spatial coherence to the different areas of the elongated space set in the glow of suspended lamps interspersed around the restaurant. Two different types of flooring enhance this, and reflect the forms on the lower level. Here the name says it all – the direct way to the bar passes through a glass portal made of champagne bottles.

A gourmet restaurant with ocean waves.

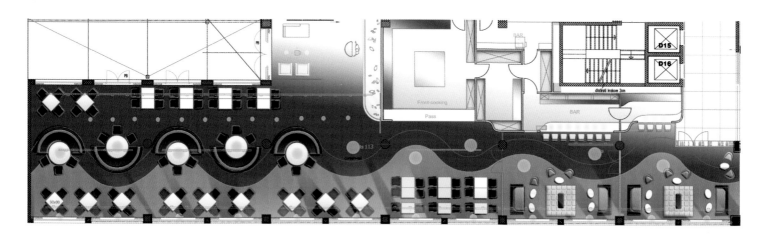

O₂ World Berlin
Germany

Steak Bar	
Category:	Upscale
Type:	Premium clientele
The Brief:	Renovation: development of a design concept for the steak bar 'the cowBOY'
Total floor space:	100.50 m²
Seats:	30
Completion:	planned for 2014

The O₂ World is a glittering magnet for the vibrant eastern district of Berlin. The Spree River is right at the front door, along with well-preserved sections of the Berlin Wall that once cut through the city and on which a host of graffiti artists and painters are immortalized. The Eastside Gallery exhibits this special part of Berlin – a city of contrasts, a colorful mix of cultures. So you're enjoying your favorite band in the Premium Area, it's intermission and you're hungry. What better place to eat than right here? The steak bar is nestled in the Premium Area and so tightly integrated into its surroundings that it seems like it's always been there. The floor plan is set asymmetrically to the corner where it's placed and greets visitors with fan-like sections. This creates a diagonally-placed bar counter directly where you pick up your food that, combined with ceiling panels placed at different angles overhead, makes for a close interlinking with the surroundings. Copper pans hang next to wooden paneling to emphasize the kitchen atmosphere where your delicious steak is prepared in minutes. And the 'wild child' eastern district of Berlin also is expressed here, since you want to know exactly where you are. A band of colorful graffiti is reference to this part of the capital.

'The cowBOY' – a steak bar with an affinity for local art.

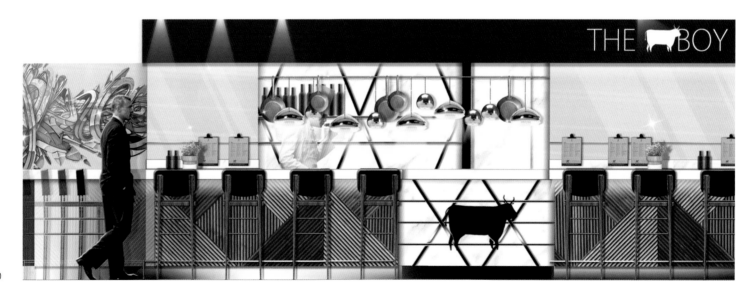

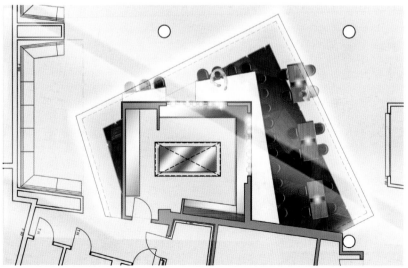

O₂ World Berlin
Germany

Cigar Lounge
Category: Upscale
Type: Premium clientele
The Brief: Renovation: development of a
design concept for the cigar lounge
Total floor space: 95 m²
Seats: 15, plus standing tables
Completion: planned for 2014

The O₂ World has an additional highlight – the smokers lounge, which is located on the same premium floor as the steak bar. While there's always time for a cigarette now and then, there are only a few places where you can retreat with a glass of cognac and enjoy a good cigar. This is the ideal place to spend time between top acts on the O₂ stage. Here you can be alone, kick back and relax – behind glass so that the smoke doesn't bother others, but also set apart far enough from the hustle-bustle so you can really enjoy yourself.

Of course, the design is all in brown tones – you can literally smell the cigars and cognac here – but combined with a small gallery of pictures as reminders of where you are and as a source for reflection. Here as well, spatial boundary is provided by diagonal shapes as a unifying element. Placed outside the room, these slats hide a bit more of what's going on inside, offer protection and communicate the premium nature of this location from afar.

A little bit of Havana for Berlin.

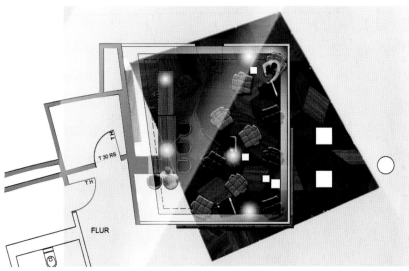

One of a Kind Hotel Vienna
Austria

Lobby

Hotel Category: ★ ★ ★ ★ ★ luxury
Hotel Type: City hotel
Size: 213 rooms
The Brief: Restructuring: development of a design concept for the lobby
Total floor space: 223.80 m²
Seats: 39

So much history! Such splendor! Vienna signifies tradition and style and remains one of the most culturally important cities in Europe. The Opera, the Opera Ball, the New Year concert, for which even the Viennese have difficulty obtaining tickets, the museums, the cathedral; the list goes on and on. So every year, Vienna attracts many visitors with an interest in culture and history from all over the world and there are still a few treasures among the hotel properties. We have such a treasure here, although showing its age a little and waiting to be reawakened with a kiss.

As expected, the revival of these old, dignified premises follows tradition, but with flair. The guest enters a multi-story lobby that radiates modern elegance. Viennese charm in black and white, with a certain extra something. A closer look at the wall covering behind the concierge station reveals a pattern composed of different dog silhouettes. At once elegant and intriguing.

Tradition meets modern design – a journey of exploration begins.

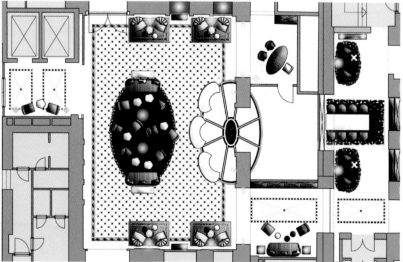

One of a Kind Hotel Vienna
Austria

Day Bar
Hotel Category: ★ ★ ★ ★ ★ luxury
Hotel Type: City hotel
Size: 213 rooms
The Brief: Restructuring: development of a design concept for the day bar
Total floor space: 146.20 m²
Seats: 45

This is where guests meet for high tea. A welcome break after a stroll through the city or a museum tour, because sightseeing can be very strenuous. Soft piano music in the background, a gently creaking parquet floor overlaid with carpets and many comfortable seating options, where guests can catch their breath and take the weight off their feet. This is what is needed; a pause between activities. Perhaps the friendly waiter will recommend one more piece of cake, making the stay perfect.

The day bar is precisely tailored to these needs and responds with warm tones. A touch of black and white from the lobby can be recognized on the walls. And another surprise follows closer inspection. Here it's the outlines of elegantly clad society ladies in the gowns that are still worn at the Opera Ball. But our bar is also equipped for the evening or a cocktail in the meantime. The long bar or the deep seating alcoves, where guests can review the day's events with friends or business associates, are inviting.

A place for many occasions – a bar with numerous faces.

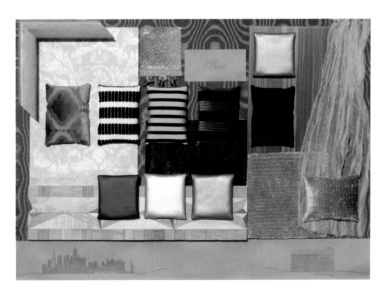

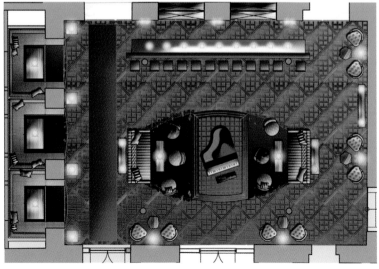

One of a Kind Hotel Vienna
Austria

Specialty Restaurant
Hotel Category: ★ ★ ★ ★ ★ luxury
Hotel Type: City hotel
Size: 213 rooms
The Brief: Restructuring: development of a design concept for the specialty restaurant
Total floor space: Restaurant 248 m², buffet 19.10 m²
Seats: 107

The property: the building's thick walls, tall rooms and ideal location give flair to this new luxury hotel. To sense the history, preserve tradition and revitalize it, that was the challenge. It quickly became clear that the restaurant must be relocated to the exterior and the activity on the street. A little see and be seen is also important in the luxury segment. However, the greatest benefit of this restructuring is the separate entrance. There is simply nothing worse for a hotel restaurant than a long approach through the lobby, in full view of the receptionist and the other guests. Fear of entering stops half of the potential guests and they never reach the restaurant.

The basic conditions are in place and the design wraps the space in a tonally subdued color scheme that puts the guest in a pleasant, calm mood from the first glance. The mix of black and white ensures continuity with the other areas.

Viennese chic in cream, black, and white.

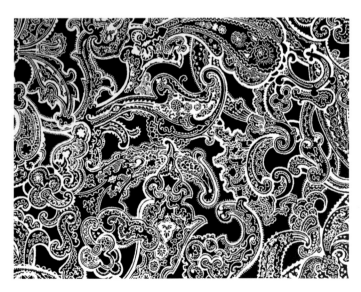

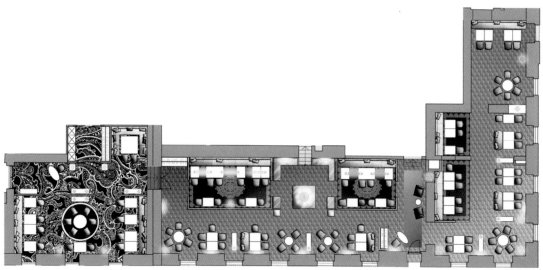

Palais Maxi Munich
Germany

Champagne Bar
Hotel Category: ★ ★ ★ ★ ★ superior
Hotel Type: City hotel
Size: 300 rooms
The Brief: Renovation: development of a design concept for the champagne bar
Total floor space: 121 m²
Seats: 61

Close to the Munich Opera House and at the center of the premium shopping district of the Bavarian capital on the Isar River – this established luxury hotel is getting a new bar. People can be reluctant to enter a hotel bar if they aren't staying there. So the new bar should have its own, separate access to avoid this and attract more customers. A new place in the city to have fun – in the evening after your meeting, after a shopping tour or sightseeing, the perfect place to refuel and refresh. Selected for this was the former Rose Room that was completely renovated and now graces Munich's nightlife in a new suit of clothes. Prestigious, elegant, charming – these were the design objectives here.

Embedded in outer structure of the original room were ovals containing flower motifs, which were integrated into the new interior design concept. In fact, the spatial feel here is dominated by a play of oval geometric forms. Here prickling bubbles seem to rise in a glass of fine champagne, over there they seem to mix and intertwine. High-quality marble, a chandelier made of rose blossoms hanging from the ceiling – the motif of the rose can be felt everywhere. And naturally a play of colors in champagne, beige and gold tones helps create the right mood for a night of fun to come.

Elegant surroundings for a sparking drink.

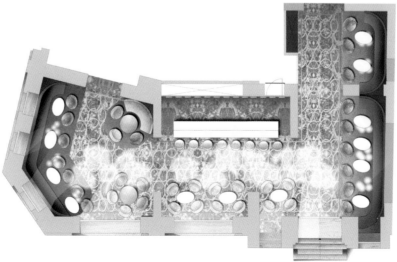

Palais Maxi Munich
Germany

Fine Dining Restaurant
Hotel Category: ★ ★ ★ ★ ★ superior
Hotel Type: City hotel
Size: 300 rooms
The Brief: Renovation: development of a design concept for the fine dining restaurant
Total floor space: Restaurant 183 m², buffet 36.50 m²
Seats: 120

Like a tender pedal in the wind – the gourmet restaurant in this tradition-rich luxury hotel should get a new face. Menu and service are the best there is, but the interior design had aged a bit and needed refreshing. While creating the new interior it became clear what the overall design theme should be – the interior should engage in a dialog with the rose as leitmotif between aperitif and main course, dessert and digestif.

Guests are immersed in a world of delicate flower pedals. Suspended lamps shaped like trumpet flowers and tables below finely-veined like foliage. Even bench and seat backs have rose shapes to grace the room. On the walls is fine chinaware. In the past there were valuable copper engravings here, now these are translated as porcelain reliefs – a room trimmed in history, fine and discreet, in a harmony of colors that combine to create a new chapter in the tradition of this hotel.

The name of the rose – a restaurant inspired by flowers.

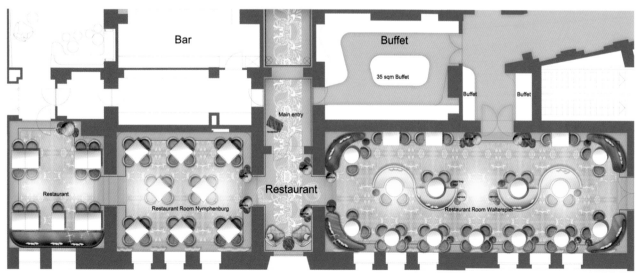

Park Inn Krakow
Poland

Lobby / Reception
Hotel Category: ★ ★ ★ ★
Hotel Type: Urban hotel
Size: 162 rooms
The Brief: New building: development of a design concept for the reception
Total floor space: 177 m^2
Seats: 6
Detailed design & sight supervision: Ovotz design Lab.
Boutique Media: Boutique Design Award 2009, category 'Best Futuristic Design Scheme' Adex Platinum Award 2010

A new hotel in Poland for this dynamic brand. The building's design aspirations are already visible on the outside. With its tapering, rounded details, the building represents a new generation, boldness and innovation. It makes a clear statement and shows the importance of this location. Businessmen and tourists meet here and expect contemporary, uncomplicated service and appropriate design.

Outside in. The interior design is in direct dialog with the architecture. The dominant vocabulary of the six-story building is carried over to public areas in the interior. Reception welcomes its guests with a spatial sculpture reminiscent of the architecture that points toward the interior. Formally, it is created by both the desks and a gateway that leads us to the elevator. A grand gesture. At once inviting and future oriented. And the surroundings join in. Walls, floor and ceiling carry the lines into the interior. Isolation of this extravagant form is prevented and the formal language is extended into adjacent areas.

From the outdoors to the inside: interior design as a response to the built form.

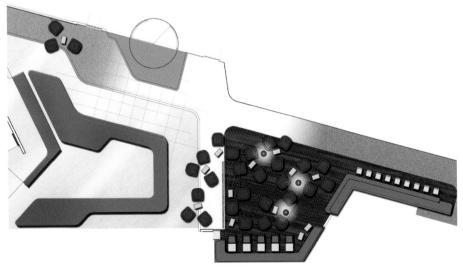

Park Inn Krakow
Poland

Lobby Bar
Hotel Category: ★ ★ ★ ★
Hotel Type: Urban hotel
Size: 162 rooms
The Brief: New building: development of a design concept for the lobby bar
Total floor space: 85 m²
Seats: 40
Detailed design & sight supervision: Ovotz design Lab.
Boutique Media: Boutique Design Award 2009, category 'Best Futuristic Design Scheme' Adex Platinum Award 2010

The bar as pivot point. Here, the hotel guest can begin by enjoying a coffee, followed by an aperitif in the evening and an after-dinner drink. The atmosphere of the hotel bar can influence the mood. If a guest does not feel well looked after here, the hotel stay is quickly called into question. Seats at the bar and conversation with the bartender are important. But the quality of other seating must also be suitable. Guests can be seen by strangers and can observe them just as easily. One either wishes to be seen or remain undisturbed. It should be remembered that many more women travel these days and these issues take on new importance.

This bar responds to their needs, providing alcoves for those who prefer intimacy and open seating for those who want to be 'on show'. The location shows its colors and very clearly identifies the area for encounters. Red and orange tones define the rules and stand out emphatically from the setting, which otherwise employs the reception area vocabulary.

To see or to be seen, that is the issue here.

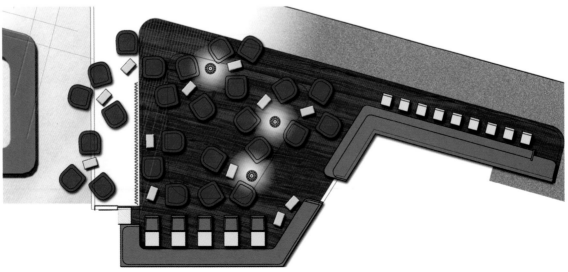

Park Inn Krakow
Poland

Restaurant
Hotel Category: ★ ★ ★ ★
Hotel Type: Urban hotel
Size: 162 rooms
The Brief: New building: development of a design concept for the restaurant
Total floor space: 204.20 m²
Seats: 116
Detailed design & sight supervision: Ovotz design Lab.
Boutique Media: Boutique Design Award 2009, category 'Best Futuristic Design Scheme' Adex Platinum Award 2010

Capacity for change is particularly important in a hotel restaurant. Evenings require a completely different atmosphere from mornings. In the evening, guests wish to conclude the day. Mornings should motivate for the activities that lie ahead. The balancing act lies in satisfying the need for clarity, orientation and privacy. Acoustics also play a part. Overhearing a conversation at a neighboring table can be disturbing and may cause guests to feel that the personal discussion at their own table is not completely private. Again, women should be kept in mind. They travel in increasing numbers and pay close attention to these criteria.

This restaurant solves the problem by working with many different materials. Semi-transparent panels provide visual and acoustic privacy. A guest feels comfortable in the evening, even though the restaurant is busier in the mornings. Various lighting settings support different scenarios. And the restaurant picks up the bar color scheme, which is still visible in the next room. The basic color varies and is accompanied by patterns and warmer berry accents.

Orange meets blackberry – a restaurant shows its colors.

158

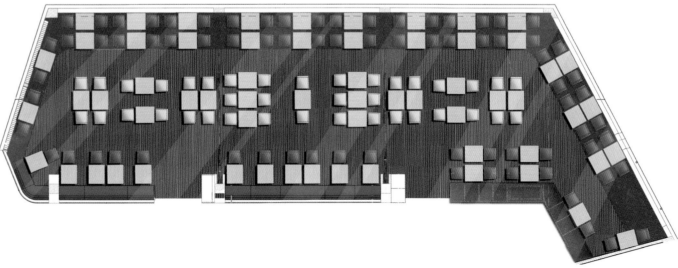

PrimeView Restaurant Zurich
Switzerland

Gourmet Restaurant
Category: Luxury
Type: Business guests, city tourists
The Brief: New building: development of a design concept for the gourmet restaurant
Total floor space: 210 m²
Seats: 86

The location of the tower and the restaurant on its top floor provides a phenomenal view over Zurich and the lake with its scenery and mountain backdrop. The entire floor is dedicated to catering and the fine dining restaurant focuses on local specialties with an accompanying selection of wines. The full-height, wrap-around glazing provides every seat with its own completely individual view across the city's rooftops.

The interior appears in elegant cream nuances accompanied by a fine, dark parquet floor overlaid with islands of carpet. There is a small lounge area at the entrance for an aperitif and various seating options in the restaurant. Diners may either sit on small sofas, at tables for two or four, or on the long banquette. And most important! An integrated band of mirror above the banquette also allows a dinner companion to enjoy some of the mountain view. Different pendant lamps give structure to the space but do not restrict visibility. Thus, the view of the illuminated wine cabinet remains unobstructed and the next selection can already start to swirl around in the imagination.

Enjoyment above the rooftops of Zurich.

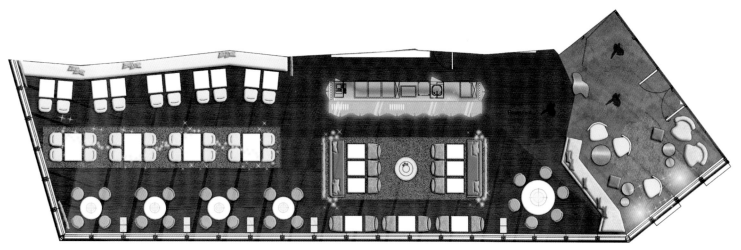

PrimeView Restaurant Zurich
Switzerland

Bistro
Category: Luxury
Type: Business guests, city tourists
The Brief: New building: development of a design concept for the bistro
Total floor space: 216.60 m²
Seats: 126

The bistro is attached to the specialty restaurant and serves light meals and snacks. Exactly like next door, it is the breathtaking view through the full height windows that makes the location truly special. This is the place to experience Zurich, to experience Switzerland! The brief: offer authenticity without allowing the interior design to compete with the view.

The solution: the design defers to the scenery. The room presents itself in a slightly darker shade of light brown rather than cream. Chairs, tables, floor and lamps are all in wood to symbolize Swiss tradition and history. The rear wall is one shade darker, to serve as a frame. An abstract silhouette of the city is positioned in front of the wall. The black and white feels good; it brings freshness. Sloping planes on cabinet fronts and the ceiling reflect the outline of mountain peaks in the distance. And every seat has a good view. Seating at the bar and adjacent long tables is elevated so everyone has a view of the alpine panorama.

Natural wood with an oil finish; a modern interpretation of Switzerland.

162

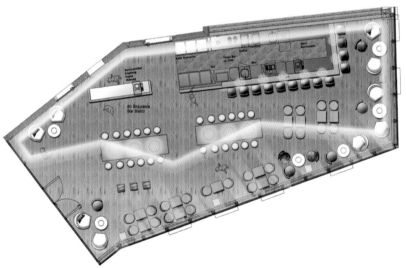

PrimeView Restaurant Zurich
Switzerland

Nightclub
Category: Luxury
Type: Business guests, city tourists
The Brief: New building: development of a design concept for the nightclub
Total floor space: 104.20 m^2
Seats: 49

The ideal spot for a nightcap to bring a strenuous business day to an agreeable conclusion or after dining in the adjoining specialty restaurant. The nightclub, where guests can first enjoy an elegantly served fine wine and later shake a leg on the dance floor. A DJ will be spinning the discs and the area in front of the bar becomes a dance floor. Panoramic glazing is repeated at the rear of the tower and the view of the night sky and city lights is equally exciting. How does the interior respond? A mix of tradition and high-tech defines the ambience. Classic designer furnishings stand alongside cubic reflective side tables. The colors are all dark with metallic finishes, accompanied by dark brown parquet and soft carpeting. Black Swarovski crystals sparkle in competition with the shimmering wall covering surface. And the eye catcher, which is also visible from the street below; changing colors from lighting troughs at the walls and ceiling, which give the room a difference atmosphere, depending on the event.

Zurich by night: dancing in the lights of the city.

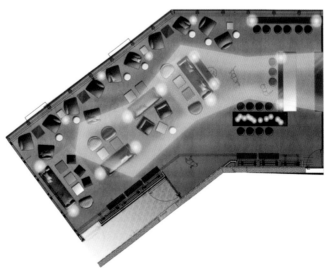

Private Hunting Lodge
Frankfurt M., Germany

Lobby & Bar
Hotel Category: ★ ★ ★ ★ ★ superior
Hotel Type: Convention and resort hotel
Size: 145 rooms
The Brief: Renovation: development of a design concept for the lobby and bar
Total floor space: Lobby 216.80 m², bar 320.50 m²
Seats: Lobby 18, bar 48

In the countryside a short distance outside Frankfurt, overlooking an idyllically situated pond. This is the site of a former manor house that was converted to a hotel years ago and has since hosted wedding parties and other family festivities in addition to conferences and weekend wellness visitors. The location enjoys perfect privacy but is easy to reach. A popular hunting estate at one time, today golf is the preferred game, followed by an evening spent with friends and a fine red wine around the fireplace in this former hunting lodge.

Complete renovation restructured the meeting areas and the large ballroom, but the interior recognizes its historic origins –

combined with contemporary elements, of course. The reception desk and bar behind it enclose the back-of-house area with an organic, dynamic form, creating an interior link to the water in front of the building. They nestle elegantly within the natural environment and yet the choice of solid surface material demonstrates that they originate in the present century. At the rear are curving wood slats, which take advantage of the high space and enclose an additional lobby area above.

Hunting belongs to the past – the hotel as new social rendezvous.

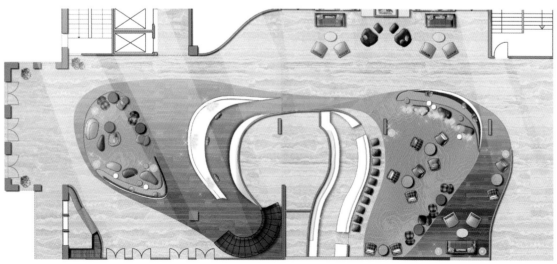

Radisson Blu Hamburg Airport
Germany

Lobby / Reception
Hotel Category: ★ ★ ★ ★ superior
Hotel Type: Airport hotel
Size: 266 rooms
The Brief: New building: development of a design concept for the reception area
Total floor space: 355 m²
Seats: 17
Adex Platinum Award 2011

A challenge: a circular floor plan for the hotel and many simultaneous demands on the reception level. The guest reaches the lobby directly from the airport and in a single space finds not only reception, but also access to the floors, elevators, conference rooms and ballroom. The bar and restaurant are on the same level, together with prefunction spaces for the meeting areas. The solution? Different ovals play off against the center by consciously departing from the circular geometry and relieving its rigidity. After all, people are not symmetrical and would never fit these constraints. The layout adapts to the user. Different functions take place in different ovals. The reception desks appear separately as freestanding ports of call for personal interaction with guests. I'm not a number here and receive personal attention. In this case, form is also defined by the oval; wood intersected by a glass cube.

A lobby and the squaring of the circle.

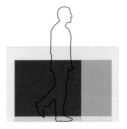

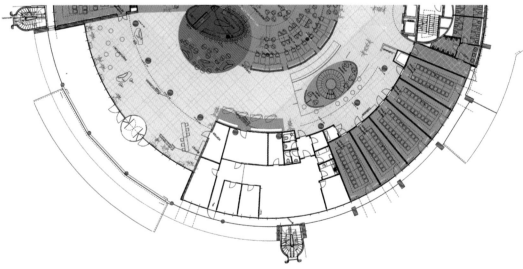

169

Radisson Blu Hamburg Airport
Germany

Bar

Hotel Category: ★ ★ ★ ★ superior

Hotel Type: Airport hotel

Size: 266 rooms

The Brief: New building: development of a design concept for the bar

Total floor space: 79 m²

Seats: 35

Adex Platinum Award 2011

With its direct connection to the airport, many guests use the bar for a conference shortly before their departure. A quick situation update, a short meeting summary, or simply a coffee in relaxed surroundings with a business partner who hasn't been seen for a long time. The bar as first port of call in the hotel and entrance to the restaurant. The concept: centrally placed in the circular floor plan, it presses in with its oval shape. Anchored by a column, it doesn't stand out from events, but very naturally becomes an integral element. Circulation routes and business activity all around. This is the place to see and be seen. Yet guests don't feel they are in a goldfish bowl. It all blends quite informally. The casually placed seating is welcoming and does not feel bulky. Informal proximity is possible here, face to face or back to back. A bar that isn't too self-important and is still a magnet for communication.

An energetic reception area – the oval within the circle.

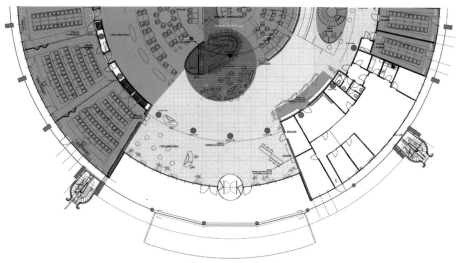

Radisson Blu Hamburg Airport
Germany

Restaurant

Hotel Category: ★ ★ ★ ★ superior

Hotel Type: Airport hotel

Size: 266 rooms

The Brief: New building: development of a design concept for the 'Filini' restaurant

Total floor space: Restaurant 332 m², buffet 45,6 m²

Seats: 164

Adex Platinum Award 2011

A restaurant at the hub of activity. Centered in the circular reception hall as a meeting place for breakfast, conference breaks, business lunch or a relaxed evening dinner. For large groups at times, at other times just for enjoyment by two. The challenge: guests pass by on the way to their rooms. Stimulate interest and provide privacy at the same time, that's the brief.

The interior design solves this with various room dividers. Crescent-shaped slabs separate areas so conferences can quietly take place alongside hotel dining. A shimmering, semi-transparent curtain functions as a separation from the primary circulation axis. In addition to partial transparency that stimulates curiosity, it offers privacy and an improvement in room acoustics. If necessary, it can be moved to one side to provide flexibility for events. There is a further highlight at the rear. The buffet area attracts attention with lighting effects and, if it is no longer needed, can be closed off in the evening as a room within a room.

An emphasis on flexibility – the multifunctional restaurant.

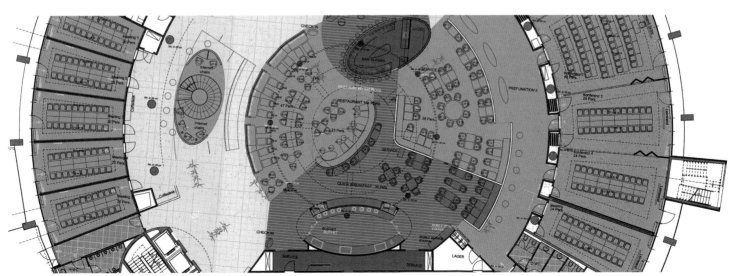

Schlösschen Löwenstein
Albersweiler, Germany

Restaurant
Category: Gourmet restaurant
Type: Business and conferences clients
Size: 42 rooms
The Brief: Renovation: development of a design concept for restaurant areas across two levels
Total floor space: Restaurant 83 m², buffet 23 m²
Seats: 44

Constructed in 1764, this former administration building from the age of the Holy Roman Empire offers ample space for conferences, meetings and fine dining. The project saw the creation of new restaurant areas with adjoining buffet zones on the ground and upper floors. The main restaurant is located on the ground floor and opens directly onto the park to the rear of the building. Entering the restaurant, guests will be drawn naturally towards this attractive green vista as they let go of their cares and relax. Inspired by the neighboring conference center, the restaurant's design concept takes its cue from the building's natural surroundings. 'Greenfield dining' follows 'greenfield thinking', and the untreated materials and warm canon of colors throughout are pleasing to the eye. The centerpiece – the dialog between the interior and the lush greenery of the park landscape outside underscores the visual appeal of this design. Large pendant lights float beneath the ceiling, lending structure and delimiting the quiet zones. Take a break in stimulating surroundings.

A dining experience like a walk in the park.

174

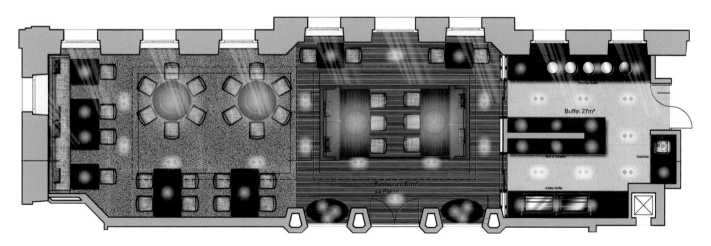

See Perle Kampen
Sylt, Germany

Lobby & Reception
Hotel Category: ★ ★ ★ ★ ★ luxury
Hotel Type: Resort hotel
Size: 46 rooms
The Brief: Renovation: development of the design concept for the lobby with reception area
Total floor space: 72 m²
Seats: 7

This extension will welcome guests to a hotel with a rich history. High ceilings characterize the new reception zone, creating a bright and spacious atmosphere where the measured influence of tradition unites the old with the new. What sets this hotel apart from its peers? Its character, personality and dedication to individuality. Communicating these values with a new design proved to be a complex challenge with a simple solution. This patchwork concept blends the aesthetics of yesterday with today, the rough with the smooth, the soft with the hard, nature and artifice, the vivid and the neutral... Full-length flat panels with a range of finished surfaces structure the room, ready to take in new tales and pass them on to future generations of travelers. Contemporary furniture sits alongside the vintage and new flooring borders older surfaces while modern lighting elements illuminate the room. It's a concept for guests keen to blaze a trail into the future without forgetting the splendor of things past. The hotel's seated check-in service is a model of discretion and sets the mood for an experience that invites guests to lean back and forget about their cares.

Where the past meets the future – a patchwork of the ages.

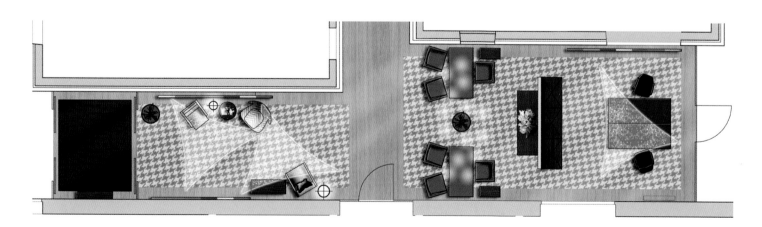

Sky Tower Berlin
Germany

Sky Bar & Club
Hotel Category: Luxury
Hotel Type: City hotel
Size: 350 rooms
The Brief: New building: development of a design concept for the signature bar with club
Total floor space: 606.90 m²
Seats: 173

The operators of this luxury hotel in central Berlin realized from the outset that laying the foundations for success was a matter of standing out among the numerous other luxury hotels recently established in the metropolis or currently in development. The time was ripe for something new, a project with the personality and history that would delight guests with its story and authenticity. Hotels haunted by design concepts bereft of real spirit are a dime a dozen. Today's urban nomads are hungry for inspiration and emotional experience.

Inspiration was found in the heydays of the German capital close to one hundred years ago: the Charleston. An era, a dance and life lived to the fullest. From its central location, the Sky Bar offers panoramic views across the cityscape from its perch at the summit of this modern tower. How could the interior possibly compete with this stunning backdrop? There's only thing to do: let your light shine. The result – a bar where guests dance in the company of icons from ages past and contemporary furnishings, a place to outshine everything the city has to offer.

1920s Berlin re-imagined – Charleston for the 21st century.

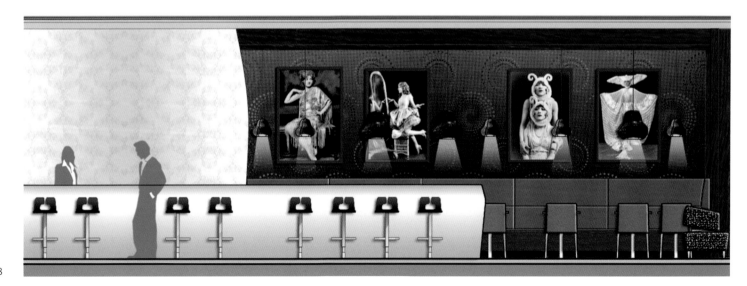

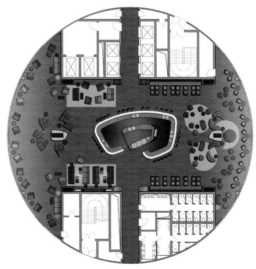

Stadtpalais Leipzig
Germany

Lobby & Reception
Hotel Category: ★ ★ ★ ★ ★ luxury
Hotel Type: City hotel
Size: 177 rooms
The Brief: Restructuring / conversion: development of a design concept for the lobby with reception area
Total floor space: 69.10 m²
Seats: 6

A historical palace at a central location in Leipzig finds a new lease on life as a beautiful hotel. The task: to create a lobby that will offer guests a warm welcome and breathe life into the building's historical substance. Seeking inspiration, we turned to the past and stumbled upon Bach, Goethe, Auerbach's Cellar and books, books, books – this is the home of the famous Leipzig Book Fair and numerous publishing houses. Books are destined to play a major role here, accompanying today's urban nomads as travel guides from one journey to the next.

Our reception desk is home to some essential reading: a massive bound volume overflowing with information about the surrounding city. Permanently ensconced in the middle of the counter's long sweeping line, it waits close to hand with plenty of tips for newcomers, insiders and those aspiring to join the club. The lobby's ambience reflects its historical location: fabric wall coverings, chandeliers and the sumptuous pattern of the carpeting reflects the charm of days past. The counter steals the show with new materials and surfaces combined with a gold finish that unites the past and present.

A lobby to unite the past and present – the future awaits.

Stars Zurich
Switzerland

Lobby & Bar
Hotel Category: Individual
Hotel Type: City hotel
Size: 220 rooms
The Brief: New building: development of a design concept for the lobby and bar
Total floor space: 258 m²
Seats: 84

A design with its sights set firmly on a younger clientele that picks and chooses accommodation online through social media, smartphones and tablets. Step one: check out hotel reviews online. Step two: check in. Step three: upload holiday pics. Click, click, click. The lobby is spacious, flexible and multi-functional in design.

At its heart: the reception counter, meeting place and bar. A personal concierge is always on hand to offer advice. A self-service grab-and-go refrigerator in one corner supplies guests with food and beverages around the clock – a genuine just-like-home experience. With its roaring open fire, the lounge area is a place to chill out, to check your emails or wait for your friends. For those wanting a little more in the way of communication, there is a well-stocked library of books by authors from the region. A separate room is available for small conferences and private functions. The design is unequivocally Swiss – the vocabulary, materiality and sprinkling of visual references in contemporary interpretations say it all. The result: a design that is picture perfect for a young hotel in Zurich!

The lobby rediscovered – multi-functionality goes Swiss.

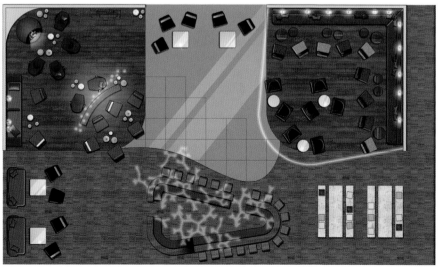

Steigenberger Hotel Bremen
Germany

Reception & Lobby Bar
Hotel Category: ★ ★ ★ ★
Hotel Type: Business hotel
Size: 137 rooms
The Brief: New building: development of a design concept for a reception area and lobby bar
Total floor space: Lobby 188 m², bar 151 m²
Seats: Lobby 24, bar 67

A new building on the banks of the Weser River: a place for the business guests to meet, share ideas and feel at ease. Guests don't have far to go for entertainment: a variety theater housed within the building complex can be accessed directly through the lobby, promising dry feet whatever the weather. The building's exterior is decidedly contemporary. Its transparent façade is all 'Zeitgeist' and technology. But there's more to this hotel than meets the eye: a scent of ocean breeze hangs in the air over the retired wharves nearby.

Breaking with the monotonous cool design of so many new high-rises, the interior draws on contemporary and historical elements, juxtaposing natural materials with technology. Rusted surfaces meet stainless steel, matt lacquer finishes and polished stone complement raw driftwood. The color scheme: a canon of brown, rust red and orange tones. Recessed lighting elements glitter like waves splashing against the quay wall. The bar forms a transition to the restaurant, where the eye-catching floor coverings make waves.

Fair sailing for business conferences – a hotel that sets its own course.

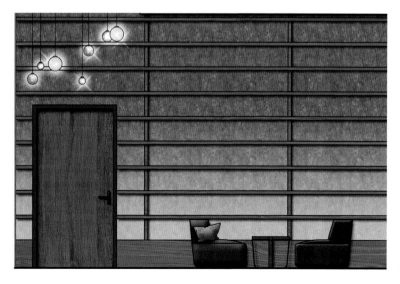

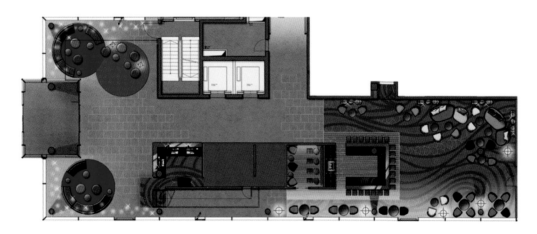

Steigenberger Hotel Bremen
Germany

Restaurant
Hotel Category: ★ ★ ★ ★
Hotel Type: Business hotel
Size: 137 rooms
The Brief: New building: development of a design concept for the restaurant
Total floor space: Restaurant 184.50 m², buffet 42 m²
Seats: 112

As a rule hotel restaurants wear several faces. Mornings they welcome one and all as the vast majority of guests prefer to breakfast in-house and then freshen up in their rooms before venturing forth into the outside world. But dining in the same room on an evening can be something of an anti-climax and many guests prefer to seek their culinary comfort in more private settings. But if a restaurant's design was versatile, what guest would pass up the opportunity to dine in-house late in the evening before slinking off to a peaceful night's rest? The solution is highly flexible design: in the morning a breakfast buffet is stocked and serviced straight from the kitchen. Come nightfall and all that has vanished. Partitions and a different lighting concept land the restaurant a more intimate feeling in the evenings, revealing eye-catching back-lit wine racks. Where were they hiding this morning? The transformation is complete, creating a cozy, welcoming atmosphere.

Dining transformed – a restaurant with a double-life.

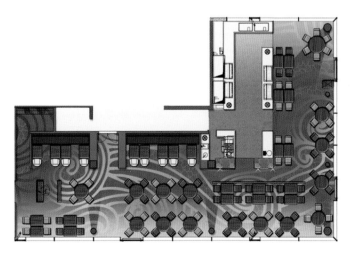

Steigenberger Grandhotel & Spa Heringsdorf, Usedom, Germany

Reception & Lobby Bar
Hotel Category: ★ ★ ★ ★ ★ luxury
Hotel Type: Resort hotel
Size: 160 rooms, 10 sea residences
The Brief: New building: development of a design concept for the reception area and lobby bar
Total floor space: Lobby 248.60 m², bar 167.80 m²
Seats: Lobby 28, bar 54

A new luxury hotel for one of the popular beach resorts on Germany's Baltic Coast. This former Imperial Spa is famous for its elegant 'Bäderarchitektur', which glows even today in radiant white, reveling in its history. The interior design is in keeping with the setting, adopting various stylistic elements yet presenting a clearly contemporary vision of hospitality. The result evokes the past while subscribing to modern design mores.

Casual elegance: the atmosphere within the lobby is reminiscent of a members-only East Coast sailing club. There is a living room ambience to the lobby, with plenty of cushions, rugs, books and a rag-tag assortment of furniture that conjures up all the pleasures of visiting an old friend. Vis-à-vis: a lobby bar that's not afraid to take center-stage. While city hotel bars need to offer their guests a sense of intimacy in the evening, guests at this beach-side resort will be keen to socialize in style after a day in the sun with their families.

Imperial elegance spiced with casual seaside chic.

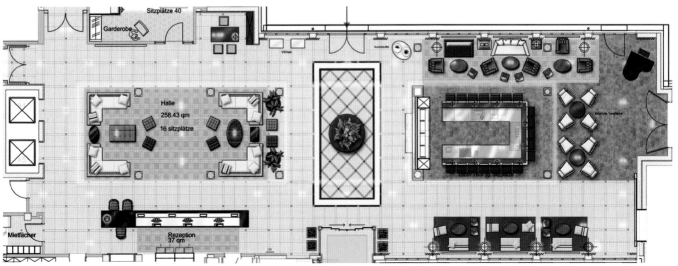

Steigenberger Grandhotel & Spa Heringsdorf, Usedom, Germany

Library & Bar

Hotel Category: ★ ★ ★ ★ ★ luxury

Hotel Type: Resort hotel

Size: 160 rooms, 10 sea residences

The Brief: New building: development of a design concept for the library and bar

Total floor space: 102 m²

Seats: 32

What could possibly top a leisurely day's reading on the beach, followed by an aperitif at the lobby bar, a round of see-and-be-seen and a sumptuous meal surrounded by verdant greenery on the terrace? A nightcap at a first-class bar with a warm and cozy atmosphere, of course. When the evening chill sets in, there's nothing quite like a sophisticated cognac, brandy or bitters with some nibbles on the side and a game of chess or backgammon. Not to mention good conversation in pleasant company! A glass séparée furnished with wing chairs beckons for those wishing to indulge in a cigar without disturbing other guests...

The bar oozes with the refined ambience of an English gentlemen's club – it's simply perfect for five o'clock tea! Warm, dark tones, paintings, books and subdued lighting prevail. Midnight blue and warm red tones together with dark woods set the mood for a dignified conclusion to a hard day's relaxation, inviting guests to reflect on the day's events as they make plans for tomorrow...

English flair on the Baltic – a bar that defines relaxation.

190

191

Steigenberger Grandhotel & Spa Heringsdorf, Usedom, Germany

Bistro

Hotel Category: ★ ★ ★ ★ ★ luxury

Hotel Type: Resort hotel

Size: 160 rooms, 10 sea residences

The Brief: New building: development of a design concept for the 'Waterfront Bistro & Bar'

Total floor space: Interior 185.60 m², exterior 295.30 m²

Seats: Interior 49, exterior 168

This hotel bistro opens directly onto the promenade – there, where the sound of ocean waves mingles with the scent of salt, sand and seashells. It's the perfect spot to pick up an ice cream or feast on fine seafood with champagne! Framed by a spacious wrap-around terrace, the bistro has something for everyone. Whether you prefer to stand or sit, guests are guaranteed to find like minds here.

Nothing conveys the fresh spirit of the seaside better than the color blue. Suddenly the salmon, oysters and tartare all taste that much better! Throw in a chilled glass or two

and the day is saved. The bistro's park-like ambience is destined to delight with white benches, curved armrests, warm lighting, brass lampshades, cushions and ocean views indoors and out. Nautical maps guide the way. Where will your journeys take you to next? This is a place to lay plans. Don't forget to include this refuge by the sea in yours...

Fresh food in blue – the seaside vibe up close.

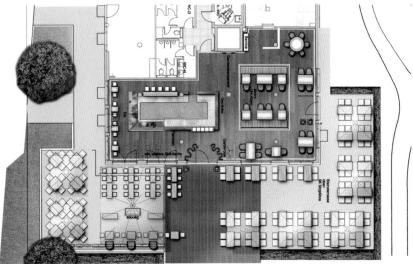

Steigenberger Grandhotel & Spa Heringsdorf, Usedom, Germany

Restaurant

Hotel Category: ★ ★ ★ ★ ★ luxury

Hotel Type: Resort hotel

Size: 160 rooms, 10 sea residences

The Brief: New building: development of a design concept for the 'Lilienthal' restaurant

Total floor space: Restaurant 472.70 m², buffet 71.90 m²

Seats: 226

What do contemporary guests desire? They inhabit a world that grows faster by the day, a world of ubiquitous access. Anytime, anywhere. 24/7: 24 hours / 7 days. Vacations are a chance to switch off, to let go of our everyday concerns, to unwind and enjoy being pampered. Time out is time well spent. Leave the anonymous, artificial world of computers with its constant stream of updates behind you. Get back to basics and go off-line – revel in reality.

Inspired by Germany's renowned 'Bäderarchitektur', the design for this restaurant draws on the vocabulary of the Imperial Spa: fine striped wallpapering, translucent white drapery, white chandeliers and an abundance of whitewashed wood – the ambience of this large-scale buffet restaurant invites guests to indulge in visions of a lost epoch. It is the perfect setting to savor the wonders that life has to offer. The sunny color canon will delight even on the grayest of days and promises an uplifting experience whatever the weather.

A restaurant with history – elegance in white on Usedom.

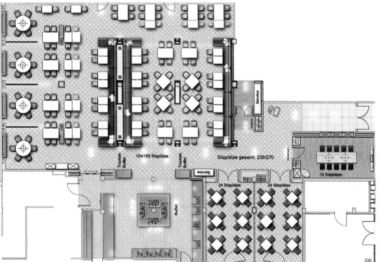

Steigenberger Grandhotel & Spa Heringsdorf, Usedom, Germany

Fine Dining Restaurant
Hotel Category: ★ ★ ★ ★ ★ luxury
Hotel Type: Resort hotel
Size: 160 rooms, 10 sea residences
The Brief: New building: development of a design concept for the 'Seaside' fine dining restaurant
Total floor space: 106.80 m²
Seats: 44

This restaurant for special occasions boasts a separate entrance, a private deck and an exclusive menu. Dining is individual and à la carte. White was de rigeur under the German Kaiser, as the island's more famous buildings testify. The setting invites guests to immerse themselves in history – switch off and enjoy. It's time to shift down a gear. Just for tonight – turn off your mobile and try to imagine how we ever managed without them...

The ambience is evocative, conjoining white and black, old and new. Mounted on a modern translation of vintage wall coverings, the empty picture frames set off the scene, stimulating the mind and inviting guests to unleash their imaginations. A hush descends from time to time as guests ponder their creations. Contemporary seating and carpeting bring us into the here and now, returning us to the modern age. That's where we want to be, but we'll come back soon!

Bäderkultur 2.0 – **elegance in black and white.**

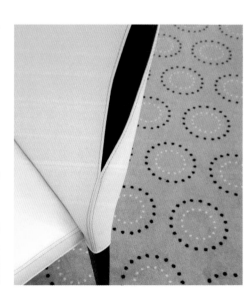

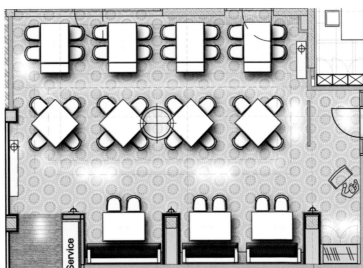

Steigenberger Hotel Hamburg City, Germany

Restaurant

Hotel Category: ★ ★ ★ ★

Hotel Type: City hotel

Size: 233 rooms

The Brief: Renovation: development of a design concept for the restaurant 'Calla'

Total floor space: Restaurant 291.30 m², buffet 103.50 m²

Seats: 110

One Michelin Star

Adex Gold Award 2011

Situated just above waterline on the hotel's so-called Fleet Floor, this restaurant enjoys a quayside view of shipping passing along the waterway at its doorstep. The challenge: to service hotel guests with a breakfast buffet each morning before taking on an entirely new guise for evening diners. After dark a private à la carte atmosphere is called for, requiring that the morning's buffet tables be banished from sight. But that's not all – cutaway ceiling sections also expose the restaurant to the hustle and bustle of the hotel lobby above.

Water defines this design, with clay tones that infuse the interior with tranquility to create a neutral stage for culinary wonders. Suspended ceiling elements lend both transparency and a sense of intimacy. The undulating lines of the hand-crafted relief mimic the dappled surface of the waterway just outside – an effect that is only heightened when the sun's rays are reflected into the interior. Droplet-shaped lighting fixtures complete the concept.

Fleet-side dining. A restaurant in motion.

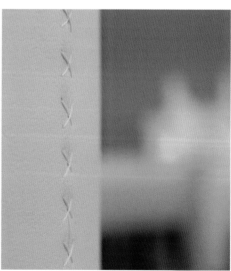

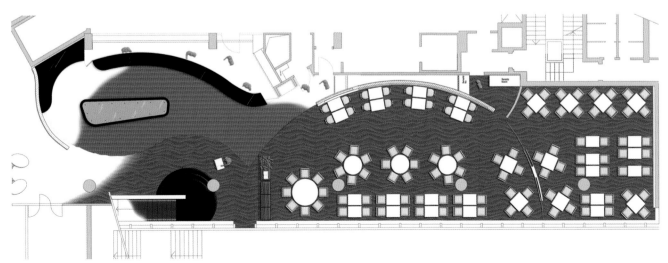

Studienhaus Albersweiler
Germany

Lobby Lounge
Category: Luxury
Type: Business and conference clients
The Brief: Extension: development of a design concept for the breakout room adjoining the conference facilities
Total floor space: 66 m²
Seats: 29

Far from the maddening crowds at head office, executives come here to think and talk outside the box. Switch off, unwind, inspire – anything is possible here. The only thing lacking was a break room: a lounge for use between meetings, a place for greenfield thinking and stimulating debate with colleagues. No sooner said than done: this new space captures the spirit and subtle repose that characterizes off-site retreats. An extension to the existing structure created space for the new lounge area, which features a range of seating options suitable for all occasions.

The multi-functional design makes the space amenable to larger meetings and discrete tête-à-têtes. Brown-beige sets the tone, coupled with and accentuated by a scattering of leather ottomans in various shades of green. This association with verdant forest is reinforced by the materiality of the leather, flooring and walls. There was no skimping on technology either: integrated laptop computers and a large flat-screen display sunk into the wall's surface allow guests to deliver small presentations and track developments in the news and stock markets.

A place for greenfield thinking.

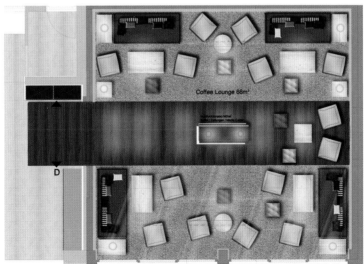

Coffee Lounge 66m²

D

Sushi House Westerland
Sylt, Germany

Specialty Restaurant
Category: Specialty restaurant
Type: Sophisticated resort clientele
The Brief: New building: development of a design concept for the sushi restaurant
Total floor space: 54.60 m²
Seats: 23

Caressed by a cool sea breeze, this North Sea island has wooed diners with freshly caught fish, shellfish and seafood specialties for decades. And yet until today sophisticated Asian flavors – prepared by a master sushi chef using only the freshest ingredients and the best that Asian cuisine has to offer – have been a rarity on these shores. This premiere fuses northern German hospitality and traditional flair with Asian flavors under the thatched eaves of a heritage structure. With just six tables, the restaurant promises a fine dining experience in an intimate atmosphere. The interior bridges the divide between the two cultures while

staying true to its roots: Traditional Nordic tiles line the wall, set above a wooden dado and ancient wooden strip flooring – once the standard in hospitality – while an ensemble of white leather armchairs, black pendant lights and carefully selected tableware sets contemporary accents and builds a bridge to the clean, minimalist aesthetics of Asian culture.

East meets West – Far Eastern delicacies complement northern German tradition.

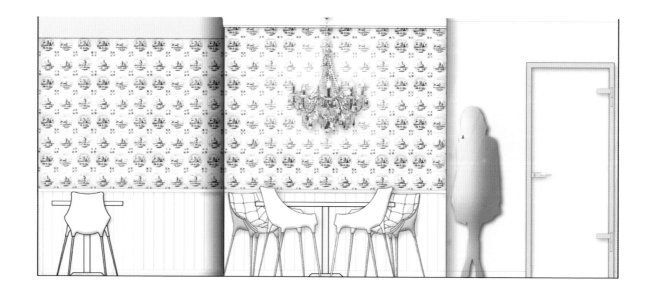

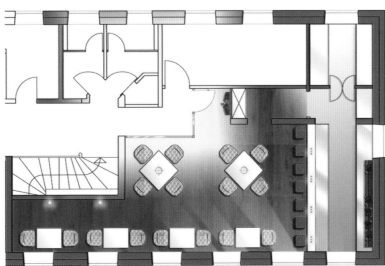

Tower 185 / PwC
Frankfurt M., Germany

Reception & Bar
Category: Upscale
Type: Business guests
The Brief: New building: development of a design concept for the reception and bar
Total floor space: Reception 21.20 m², bar 22.50 m²
Seats: 10

The challenge: this modern reception element features a bar at its rear – it is an unconventional gesture which transforms the space, inviting guests to shrug off the concerns of everyday life. After all, many a good conversation began over a refreshing drink at a bar. The bar forms a counterpoint to the clear lines of a setting that is all business. Making a statement on the location's modern currency, this unforgettable element is forward-looking, eliciting confidence with modern technologies and multifunctional design.

This flexibility is complemented by its sculptural form, positioning the element as a work of art within this space. The bar is as versatile as it is outstanding. Its organic white mass contrasts with the building's rectilinear form. An eye-catching feature reminiscent of the brain's neural network invites attention and inspires. This web-like element can be presented in a range of lighting moods, changing its character like a chameleon. A bar with a powerful visual design beckons guests to come closer and relax.

The neural network: a lobby with all the right connections.

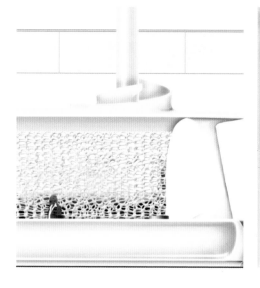

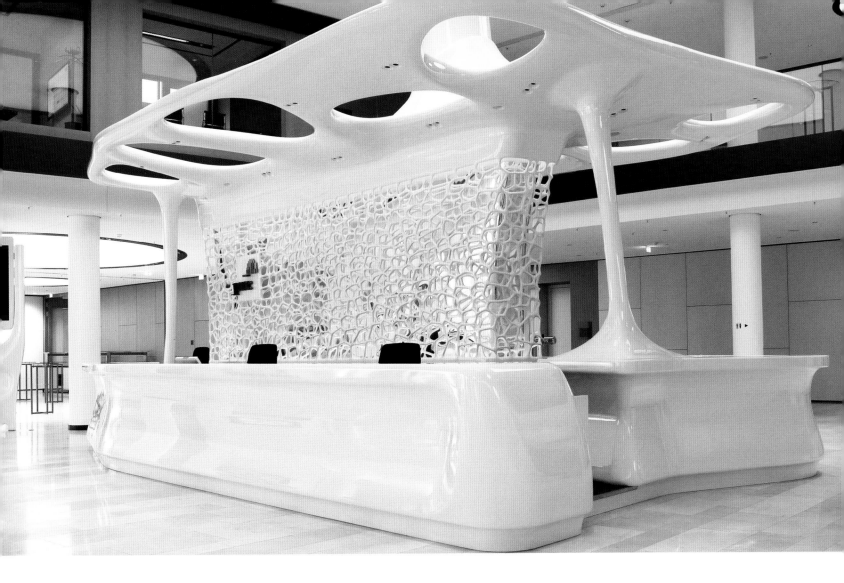

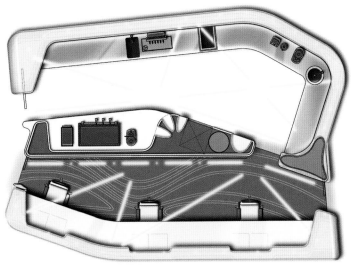

Vinothek Marburg
Germany

Bar & Restaurant
Category: Casual fine dining
Type: Business guests and tourists
The Brief: New building: development of a design concept for the wine bar and restaurant
Total floor space: 198.50 m^2
Seats: 92

Roses have always played an important role at this site – the task was to infuse this modern new building with the spirit of earlier days and create a contemporary presentation in the same moment. The challenge: developing an interior design with its ambience firmly rooted in the here and now, while cultivating a respectful attitude to the history and traditions of this location. The elegance of the building's modern clear lines sets the scene and the interior design builds on this foundation.

Nature is the central motif and the over-arching stylistic element here where the rose is at home, thriving and flourishing.

Natural stonework frames the picture, augmented by delicate formal accents in native oak and woolen fabrics. Imperceptible unless viewed from a particular angle, the rose blossoms adorning the walls and partitioning elements only surrender their secrets at a second glance – making their effect all the more charming.

In the name of the rose – fine dining under a blossom fair.

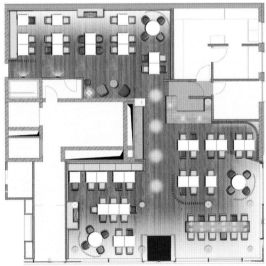

VLET Hamburg
Germany

Restaurant
Category: Gourmet restaurant
Type: Business guests and weekenders
The Brief: Conversion of a loft in the Speicherstadt district: development of a design concept for the restaurant
Total floor space: 331 m²
Seats: 105
Adex Gold Award 2010

This gourmet restaurant is situated in the heritage architecture of Hamburg's famous Speicherstadt warehouse district. Rugs, coffee beans, tea and spices imported from around the world were once stored within its walls. The site is steeped in history and represents demanding terrain for interior design. The central challenge: to preserve the authentic atmosphere without lapsing into a museality, while also revitalizing the space with contemporary elements of style. The preservation of the vaulted ceilings and steel columns quickly became cornerstones of this development – together with the installation of cutting-edge air condition-ing and lighting fixtures – ensuring that the restaurant would come up trumps with unrivalled ambience at this very special location. The original arches were restored and preserved, the steel struts stabilized – including any authentic blemishes on the ceilings and walls. Reflecting its former service as a warehouse, an unconcealed ventilation duct traverses the restaurant, while a sophisticated lighting system adds color, presenting the old and the new at their best.

History and *Zeitgeist* in one – an appealing contrast!

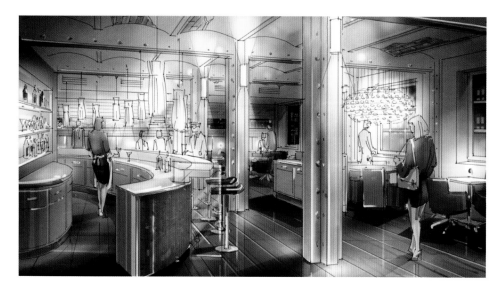

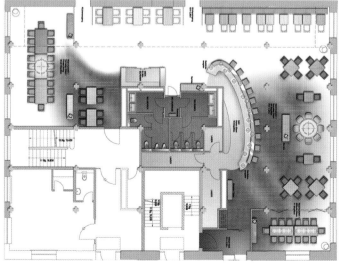

Wellness Hotel Nordheide
Germany

Lobby
Hotel Category: ★ ★ ★ ★
Hotel Type: Resort and conference hotel
Size: 52 rooms
The Brief: Revitalization: development of a design concept for the lobby
Total floor space: 251.78 m^2
Seats: 20

A house with a grand tradition set within verdant natural surroundings close to Hamburg. This hotel with a long and eventful history was given a complete facelift in a comprehensive revitalization project. The addition of conference and meeting facilities to the hotel, previously more popular as a facility for weddings and family occasions, opens the way for guests keen to do business away from the Big Smoke. With direct access to the adjoining golf course, guests can let their thoughts wander off an evening as they play their way across the green. Another highlight: extensions to the existing wellness zone enable guests to indulge in an entire battery of new therapeutic treatments.

Guests will sense the hotel's delightfully casual charm the moment they enter the lobby – an invitation to shift down a gear and relax. Wing chairs of various designs and other classical furniture elements exert their soothing influence and connect the present day interior with the hotel's past. The events of recent years are subtly present: there is plenty for guests to discover. Display cases and galleries of photographs present a range of historical details and invite guests to embark upon a journey into the hotel's past.

Take a walk down memory lane with this interior design.

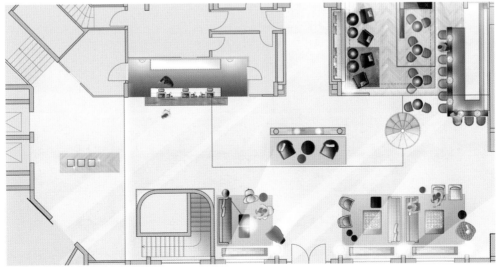

Wellness Hotel Nordheide
Germany

Bar

Hotel Category: ★ ★ ★ ★

Hotel Type: Resort and conference hotel

Size: 52 rooms

The Brief: Revitalization: development of a design concept for the bar

Total floor space: 85.80 m²

Seats: 39

After a long day with one business meeting after the next, it's time for a quiet nightcap in the discrete atmosphere of this bar. The design invites guests to linger at one of several zones – retreat to secluded environs of the rear, take a seat upstairs in the gallery, or indulge in an evening of see-and-be-seen after indulging in a solitary day in the comfort of the hotel's wellness facilities. For those seeking company, the open plan design spills over towards the lobby. The interior design builds on the mood of tranquility that defines the character of this hotel. The ambience is pure natural warmth and an exclusive atmosphere reminiscent of a private club, with a sprinkling of living-room accents. The new interior integrates a variety of anecdotes and details from the past, offering a warm and familiar welcome to regular customers, who have remained loyal to the hotel following its refurbishment. A number of vintage elements have been retained, and a large collection of photographs brings the spirit of the past to life.

An intimate atmosphere unites the past and present.

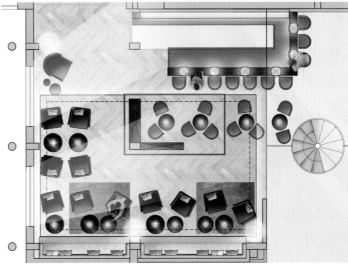

Wellness Hotel Nordheide
Germany

Specialty Restaurant
Hotel Category: ★ ★ ★ ★ ★
Hotel Type: Resort and conference hotel
Size: 52 rooms
The Brief: Revitalization: development of a design concept for the specialty restaurant
Total floor space: Restaurant 89.10 m², buffet 57.30 m²
Seats: 45

Good food is a must as guests race from conference meetings to wellness treatments and then out to the driving range to practice their stroke. Of course, some wellness guests will be hoping to lose a pound or two – and nothing could be easier! The traditional cuisine of Northern Germany is based on ingredients that are positively ideal for diners conscious of their waistlines. Responding to a diverse clientele, the restaurant exudes the same aura of credibility that characterizes its sophisticated menu – instead of international fusion cuisine and other big city fads, there is an emphasis on regional specialties and traditional fare.

Natural accents abound, defining the ambience: the entrance is marked by the graceful motion of fine wooden inlays. Quiet zones line the flanks, distinguished by their tailored furnishings. There is something for everyone: relax in an air of casual intimacy. Shelving units showcase regional products. Check-patterned fabrics are a must – this is the countryside! A scattering of classical furniture designs reminds guests of the long and venerable tradition of this house. Traditional cuisine served with a new look.

Country living – a restaurant to celebrate regional flavors.

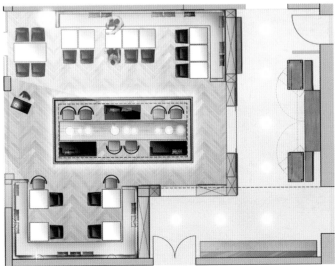

Westend Tower Zurich
Switzerland

Lobby / Reception
Hotel Category: ★ ★ ★ ★ ★ superior
Hotel Type: Luxury hotel
Size: 143 rooms
The Brief: New building: development of a design concept for the reception area
Total floor space: 297.50 m²
Seats: 37

A high-rise building for a new luxury hotel: extensive views across the city and the lake to the snow-capped mountains make the most of this location. The Swiss metropolis could not have a more spectacular backdrop. Contrasts set the tone. History and cult nightlife attractions loom large in an up-and-coming suburb built on the values of tradition and modernity. Celebrating the spirit of this popular new entertainment district, this hotel is pure Zurich – a city that never lets you forget its breathtaking natural surroundings.

The interior design: high-gloss whites bring the snow and glaciers of the rocky peaks into the interior, complemented by plenty of wood – the stuff of mountain chalets. The space is light, broad and high with beams layered in another visual reference to alpine tradition. Fine crystals glitter, evoking images of glacial ice. Chamfered silhouettes reference mountain landscapes alongside a diverse ensemble of furniture with a warm feel-good effect. The material canon – which includes untreated wood surfaces, felt, fine leather and fur – invites guests to set aside the cares of business life as they connect with their natural environment and the origins of this region.

Nature at its purest – an oasis in the Big Smoke.

Westend Tower Zurich
Switzerland

Restaurant

Hotel Category: ★ ★ ★ ★ ★ superior

Hotel Type: Luxury hotel

Size: 143 rooms

The Brief: New building: development of a design concept for the restaurant

Total floor space: Restaurant 226 m², buffet 38.30 m²

Seats: 113

Light follows shadow, just as white follows black: contrasts set off lighter shades, creating a passe-partout that brings out their contours and depth. The metropolis is a place of opposites where city lights cast their glow out into the darkness of night. Here, a restaurant offers an elegant counterpoint to the snow-capped mountains in the evening: dark tones, warm colors – from brown to black, sophisticated and oh-so elegant in the light of the chandeliers and flickering fire.

Close enough to touch, nature forms an aesthetic bridge to the design of the adjoining library: tree roots and trunks – figuring as cabinets, side tables and service furniture – are scattered throughout alongside the clear line structures in a visual response to the building's cubic form. These playful interactions accompany guests to their place at the fireside. This setting evokes a sense of privacy – the seating is casual with eye-catching fur elements as the hurly-burly of the big city gives way to nature.

White follows black – a restaurant with distinction.

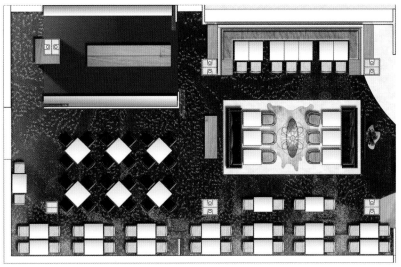

White Dice St. Petersburg
Russia

Bar & Lounge
Hotel Category: ★ ★ ★ ★
Hotel Type: Business hotel
Size: 250 rooms
The Brief: New building: development of a design concept for the bar and lounge
Total floor space: 165 m²
Seats: 54

A city with a long history, a city rich in tradition and a unique geographical location. Here visitors are surrounded by expressive design elements, ornamentation and patterns. Churches and mosques are particularly colorful here. Flowing past directly in front of the hotel is the Neva River which lends St. Petersburg its distinct vibrancy. How can a new business hotel concept assimilate all these different motifs and reinterpret them in a way that's excitingly innovative while still paying homage to the traditions of the city where it's located?

This concept answers with a floor plan that communicates movement and is dedicated to meeting the needs of guests who arrive here from around the world to gather together and communicate. The pattern created by cubes placed at different heights overhead gives a three-dimensional texture to the ceiling design – it communicates strength and, because it symbolizes the waves of water in front of the hotel, a unique sense of place as well. The materials used here reflect the colors and forms typical for Russia, rethinking their patterns and ornamentation to give a perceptible sense of culture and history. The largest cube is the bar itself, the white bar, a shimmering gathering point that adds calm and order to this world of patterns – while giving the bar its name.

A place in motion.

Young Budget Resort Mallorca
Spain

Reception

Hotel Category: Budget hotel
Hotel Type: Resort hotel
Size: 185 rooms
The Brief: New building: development of a design concept for the reception
Total floor space: 88.30 m^2
Seats: 20

A warm gentle breeze spiced with hip-hop: it's a holiday with a difference! The laptop generation, young lifestylers, urban athletes and the young at heart will all feel at home here. Guests book their stay here to save pennies, not to skimp on fun! Top-up services are available on location to satisfy your every whim.

A hands-on reception: whether you want to check your emails on the fly, check in or check out, you can do it all here! A dedicated digital communication table invites guests to network. Business centers are so yesterday – a warm and welcoming living-room flair is the name of the game these days. And if you're ever feeling clueless, one of your hosts will always be on hand to help. Most of the hotel's guests arrive fresh from the airport with self-service boarding passes in hand – after all, we like to help ourselves, whenever it suits us best.

Young Budget – a holiday with a difference.

TAKE YOUR TIME

CHECK-IN

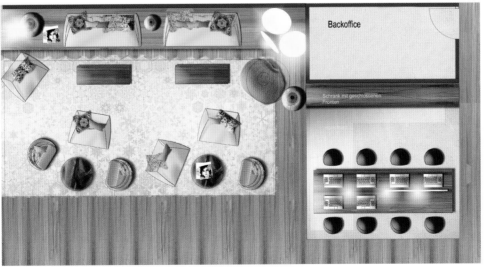

Backoffice

Schrank mit geschlossenen Fronten

Young Budget Resort Mallorca
Spain

Bar
Hotel Category: Budget hotel
Hotel Type: Resort hotel
Size: 185 rooms
The Brief: New building: development of a design concept for the bar
Total floor space: 326 m²
Seats: 90

Surfing, kiting, biking or just chilling on the beach: this resort is a place for like-minded individualists who make a lifestyle out of holidaying. Always on the go, these Web 2.0 young guns want all the comforts of home, to stay in touch with friends around the globe, to make new friends online and ... why not? ... team up with other guests for a late-night bonfire and barbecue on the beach. With its spacious lounge area, the bar is the place to be here.

The bar leads a double-life: in the daytime it's a place to drop in and refuel. Chalked up on the rear wall – all the latest news, must-dos, must-sees and a host of other useful tips. The Grab & Go refrigerators underscore the down home feeling with everything you could possibly need for a lunchtime picnic at the beach. In the evening this space is reborn: the blackboard panels slide away and the cocktail mixers come out to play... The lighting concept shifts focus, making the back-lit bar counter the center of attention.

The chameleon – a bar transformed.

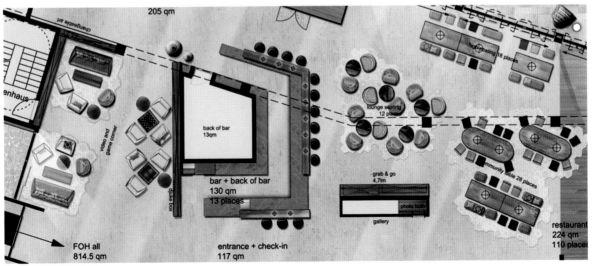

changeable art

...enhaus

video and game corner

de luxe box

back of bar
13qm

bar + back of bar
130 qm
13 places

grab & go
4,7m

photo booth

gallery

high seating 18 places

lounge seating
12 places

community table 28 places

restaurant
224 qm
110 places

FOH all
814.5 qm

entrance + check-in
117 qm

205 qm

Young Budget Resort Mallorca
Spain

Restaurant
Hotel Category: Budget hotel
Hotel Type: Resort hotel
Size: 185 rooms
The Brief: New building: development of a design concept for the restaurant
Total floor space: 360 m²
Seats: 184

A place for young urban nomads with an appetite for experience. They lead active lives and love sports as much as sunbathing. Their interests are boundless. They want to socialize, meet people, communicate. This is a place to meet and exchange ideas. A restaurant and melting pot. Laptops and tablet computers are modern travel essentials and this design delivers on their users' needs with an abundance of power outlets and the necessary seclusion for digital living.

The solution: a versatile range of seating options including a long table for socialites and private tables for couples. Feel like hanging out for a while? Try the bench seats lined with cushions or – if you're looking for something really special – a rocking chair! Relax, you're on holiday. Let your mind wander and give free rein to your imagination. This interior design is big on creativity: graffiti slogans on the walls offer food for thought and a taste of home abroad, while kaleidoscopic patterns beckon towards new horizons.

Multicultural – a restaurant with a vision.

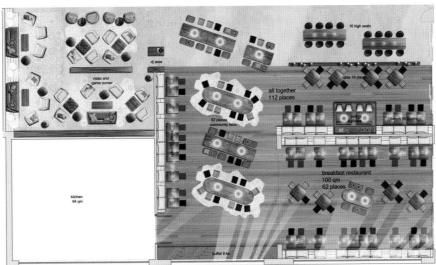

Young Budget Resort Mallorca
Spain

Outdoor F & B Outlet
Hotel Category: Budget hotel
Hotel Type: Resort hotel
Size: 185 rooms
The Brief: New building: development of a design concept for the outdoor F & B outlet
Total floor space: 155.20 m²
Seats: 60

A warm, soft breeze carries the scents of summer, sand, tanning oil and surf to our deck as the ocean waves roll in to the shore – what more could you wish for on a summer's day? Just a few meters separate the guests from the beach. Vibrant colors – all beachwear and sun umbrellas – set off the scene. Floating above, decorative string lights sway in the wind like droplets of seaspray thrown skywards by the thundering surf. A translucent screen shields this space from all too curious passers-by on the nearby promenade.

There is something for everyone: those with a more athletic sensibility can swim laps before relaxing on a soft daybed. Sun-sail cabanas offer plenty of shade for extended chill-out sessions. Hang out in a hammock or swing chair and just let your mind be free. The highlight of the evening: bonfire or barbecue? Celebrate with friends old and new – this hotel in the sun delivers a genuine soul-mate experience.

This deck shows its true colors for a real holiday feeling.

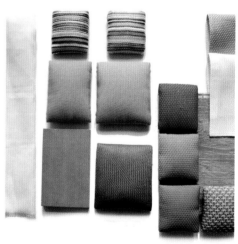

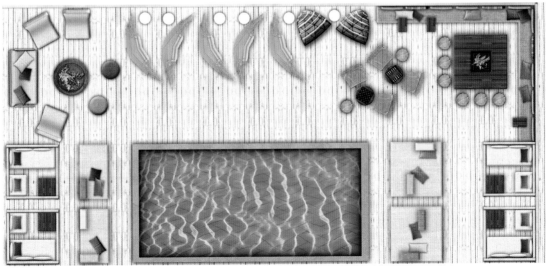

Interior Design Conception and Authors

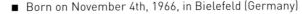

Corinna Kretschmar-Joehnk
managing director

- Born on November 4th, 1966, in Bielefeld (Germany)
- 1986 study of art history in Würzburg (Germany)
- 1987 study of interior design in Detmold (Germany) – degree (diploma) in 1993
- 1993–2000 employee at joehnk. Interior Design in Hamburg (Germany)
- Since 2000 manager of joehnk. Interior Design AG Zurich (Switzerland)
- Since 2003 managing director of JOI-Design GmbH in Hamburg (Germany)
- Since 2004 member of the BDIA (Bund Deutscher Innenarchitekten)
- 2004–2006 member of the executive committee BDIA Landesverband Küste (Germany: Hamburg, Schleswig-Holstein, Mecklenburg-Vorpommern), today engaged in the advisory board of the executive committee BDIA Landesverband Küste
- Since 2004 member of the Architectural Association Hamburg (Germany)
- Since 2007 appointment to the independent inscription committee of the interior design department in the Architectural Association Hamburg (Germany)
- Since October 2011 interior design course instructor at the University of Applied Science in Coburg (Germany)

Peter Joehnk
managing director

- Born on July 31st, 1957, in Kronach / Oberfranken (Germany)
- 1981 degree (diploma) of interior design in Kaiserslautern and Mainz (Germany)
- Since 1982 member of the BDIA (Bund Deutscher Innenarchitekten)
- 1983 distance learning degree in ecological building
- 1984 formation of his own company, joehnk. Interior Design
- 1992 university lecturer at the Muthesius art academy in Kiel (Germany)
- Since 1997 admittance as 'Member of Chartered Society of Designers' (MCSD), London
- 1998 election as professional of the IIDA (International Interior Design Association)
- 2001–2003 member of executive committee of the BDIA; delegate of the BDIA to the IFI (International Federation of Interior Designers)
- 2001 approval of the ECIA (European Council of Interior Architects)
- Since 1986 member of the Architectural Association Hamburg; since 1998 member of the Architectural Association Bavaria; since 1996 member of the Architectural Association Austria

Books published:
Raum.Werte. Creating Hospitality Design –
published in 2009 by Braun Publishing AG

101 Hotel Rooms –
published in 2011 by Braun Publishing AG

Colours for Hotels / Farben der Hotels –
published in 2013 by Callwey Verlag

- 2000–2004 served on contest committee of the Architectural Association Hamburg (Germany)
- Since 2003 manager of JOI-Design GmbH in Hamburg (Germany)
- Since 2010 appointment to the 'Konvent der Baukultur'.